How Idioms Work

Resource Book

Banks bite the bullet

The full disclosure requirement for banks to reveal their toxic assets continues to deal a severe blow to profits. Although unpopular with banks, the move was considered

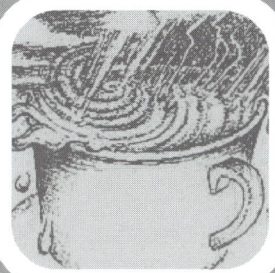

Don't be afraid to ruffle feathers

The trouble with the English is that we're too polite. We often attribute sloppy work and/or missed deadlines to a variety of unlikely excuses and even managers pre

Garnet EDUCATION

Yvonne Clarke

with illustrations by **Martin Jones**

Published by
Garnet Publishing Ltd
8 Southern Court
South Street
Reading RG1 4QS, UK

First edition published 2010.

ISBN: 978 1 85964 554 3

British Library Cataloguing-in-Publication Data
A catalogue record for this book is available from the British Library.

Production
Project manager: Kate Brown
Editorial: Kate Brown, Emily Clarke
Design and layout: Christin Helen Auth, Sarah Church, Neil Collier, Mike Hinks
Illustration: Martin Jones

The author and publisher would like to thank the following for permission to reproduce copyright material:
The Architects Journal
Bennett, Coleman & Co. Ltd.
Evening Standard
Global Trade Media
The London Daily News
The News Post Leader
North-West Evening Mail
Redactive Media Group for BIFM
Yorkshire Evening Post
Yorkshire Post
Worcester News

Every effort has been made to trace the copyright holders and we apologize in advance for any unintentional omissions. We will be happy to insert the appropriate acknowledgements in any subsequent editions.

Printed and bound
in Lebanon by International Press

In memory of my brother Christopher,
who inspired and encouraged me

Contents

Section 1   16

- bite the bullet
- a finger in every pie
- draw a line under it
- put all your eggs in one basket
- ruffle someone's feathers
- bend someone's ear
- eat your words
- make a mountain out of a molehill
- keep something under wraps
- skate on thin ice
- drag your heels
- hit the nail on the head
- keep your hair on
- an uphill struggle
- bury your head in the sand

Section 2   24

- sweep something under the carpet
- bend over backwards
- a card up your sleeve
- a spanner in the works
- break the ice
- bang your head against a brick wall
- dig your heels in
- water under the bridge
- in the hot seat
- get your wires crossed
- have a bee in your bonnet
- back to square one
- get to grips with something
- a piece of cake
- on the tip of your tongue

Section 3   32

- a chip on your shoulder
- pick holes
- splitting hairs
- left holding the baby
- over the top (OTT)
- full of hot air
- sit on the fence
- get/start the ball rolling
- jump the gun
- at the eleventh hour
- take the bull by the horns
- pay through the nose
- read between the lines
- put something on the back-burner
- down in the mouth

Section 4   40

- stick your neck out
- open a can of worms
- iron/smooth something out
- put the cart before the horse
- draw the line
- throw the baby out with the bathwater
- a big fish in a small pond
- the wrong end of the stick
- spill the beans
- play/keep your cards close to your chest
- bite someone's head off
- a hard nut to crack
- have a bone to pick
- cut corners
- nail/pin someone down

Section 5   48

- heads will roll
- a knee-jerk reaction
- hot under the collar
- have/get your ducks in a row
- money for old rope
- a fish out of water
- stick to your guns
- take the floor
- pie in the sky
- let sleeping dogs lie
- stick/poke your nose in
- two bites of/at the cherry
- a finger on the pulse
- hear something on the grapevine
- go overboard

Introduction

There are an estimated 15,000 idioms in the English language, of which at least 5,500 are in regular use. This Resource Book is for teachers whose students have already reached a good level of English (intermediate and above), but who find – not surprisingly – that idiomatic language in the workplace is confusing, or even incomprehensible. Non-native speakers at this level are often reluctant to admit that they don't understand idiomatic language, with potentially damaging consequences.

How Idioms Work illustrates in vivid, close-up imagery, a literal representation of high-frequency idioms chosen specifically for their lexical value in the workplace. The book is ideal for a) complementing functional lessons such as telephoning, emailing, meetings or business socializing; b) intensive or short-term courses; and c) as a filler or icebreaker to add fun, motivation and variety to any lesson.

How to use this book

This book has three parts:

Part A: a list of suggested activities suitable for classes, groups and one-to-one lessons.

Part B: ten sections, each comprising:

- an idioms summary page: a teacher reference and handout for the end of the lesson
- a page of illustrated idioms ('picture idioms')
- a page of written idioms
- a page of definitions

   (The layout of the illustrated idioms, written idioms and definitions are specifically designed so that they can be used back-to-back, and/or copied onto card and stored in a handy, pocket-sized format.)

- a 'Read all about it' section: invaluable for reading and consolidation, these are extracts from newspaper articles which contain contextual examples of the idioms
- a page of revision exercises, followed by a 'talking point' (in a bubble) – the origin of a selected idiom for discussion and follow-up activities

Part C

- solutions to the exercises
- templates: for adding your own idioms, brainstorming, grouping idioms of similar meaning, and compiling themed sets (for example, idioms featuring parts of the body)
- index of idioms

Tips and recommendations

1   If you are short of time, make cards from the picture idioms only. The written idioms and definitions can be left as A4 sheets.

2   The cards are designed so that if they are photocopied back-to-back, the picture idioms will have their corresponding written idioms on the reverse, or the written idioms can be copied with their corresponding definitions on the reverse.

3   Copy the idioms onto card and laminate them to create a permanent set.

4   It is possible to put idioms from throughout the book into topic-based sets, if needed.

5   Ideas for follow-up activities/homework:

   - Ask student(s) to watch a current affairs programme and make a note of idioms they hear, for discussion in the next lesson.
   - Ask student(s) to find out the commonly accepted origins of some of the phrases (see the talking points at the end of each section). One excellent website for the origins and meanings of phrases is The Phrase Finder at www.phrases.org.uk.
   - Discuss idiomatic phrases student(s) have heard in the workplace since the last lesson.
   - Look at newspapers and a) highlight/discuss idioms used in the articles; b) students try to substitute more formal phrases with idioms, or vice versa.
   - Ask student(s) to bring in the minutes of a meeting they have attended. Discuss where specific idioms have been or could have been used.
   - Student(s) make a list of idioms in their first language and discuss their possible origins, and whether there are any similarities to their English equivalents (they can use Template 4 in Part C for this).

6   At the back of this book, there are a number of blank templates. Templates 1, 2 and 3 will enable you to make your own idioms cards. Template 4 is a blank version of the idiom summary page for the student to record any new idioms. Template 5 is a mind map; students brainstorm idioms with a common key word or theme. Template 6 is a dominoes template.

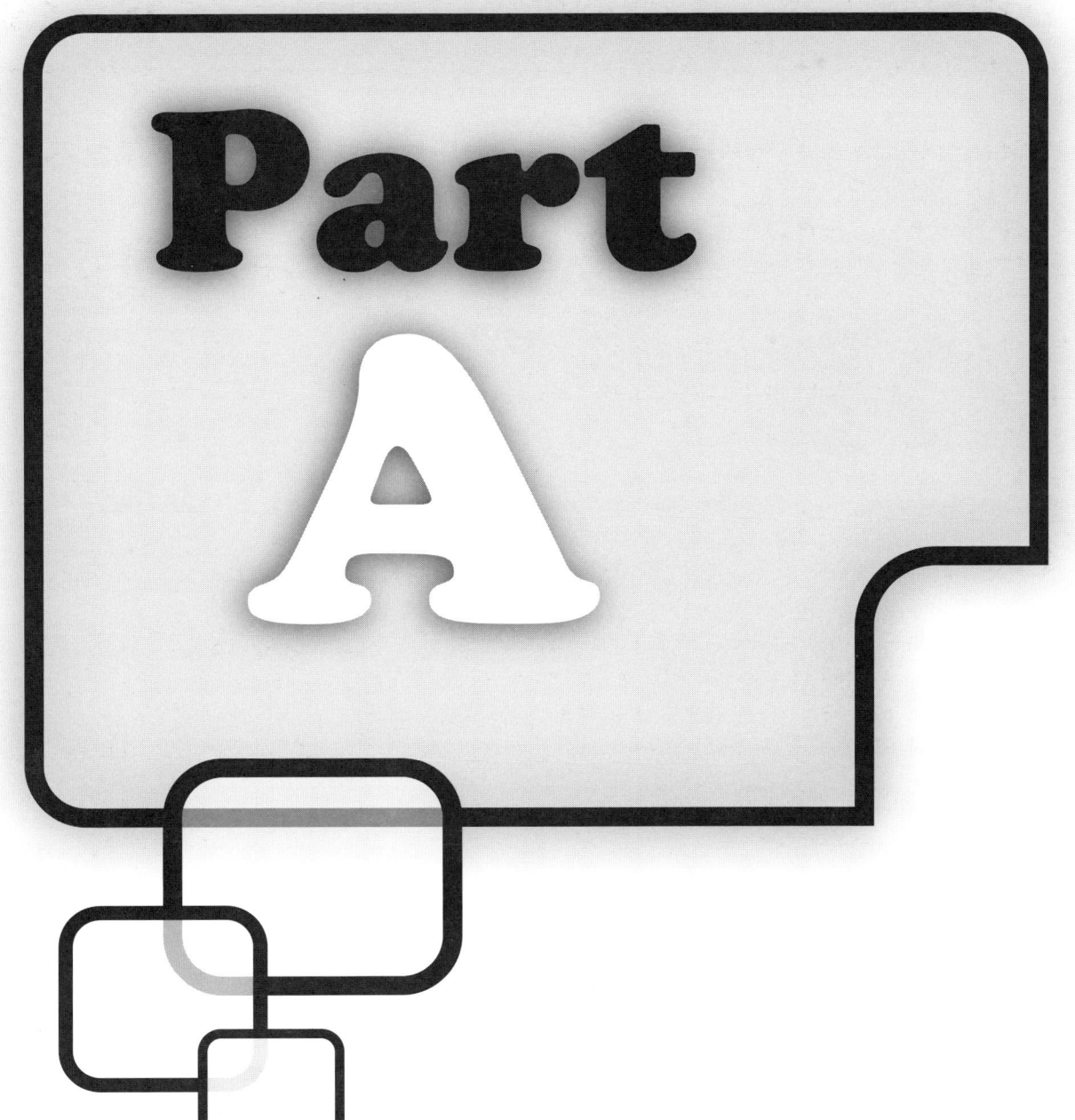

Part

A

Suggested activities

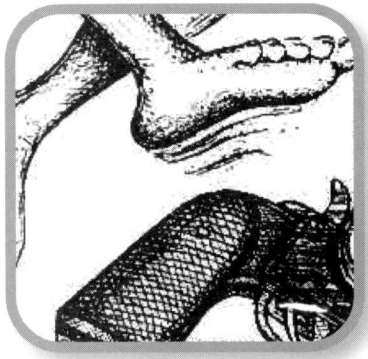

picture idiom

Jump the gun

written idiom

act before the correct time

definition

1 Picture match
- Copy and cut up picture idioms and their corresponding written idioms. Students match the idioms with the pictures.

Groups: Divide the class into teams and give each team a set of picture idioms and a set of written idioms. Teams race to be the first to match the cards.

2 Find the definition
- Copy and cut up a selection of written idioms and their corresponding definitions.
- Students match each written idiom to its definition.

Groups: as above.

3 Matching pairs
- Copy and cut up picture idioms and their corresponding written idioms.
- Split the cards into two sets; face down on the table.
- A student turns over one card at a time from the top of each pile and if they match, he/she keeps them. If not, he/she replaces them anywhere in the two sets of cards.
- The winner is the student with the most pairs of matching cards.

4 Memory game
- Copy and cut up picture idioms and their corresponding written idioms.
- Shuffle the cards and place them face down in two sets (five rows of three cards).
- Students take turns to pick up one card simultaneously from each set and decide whether they match.
- If the two cards match, they keep them. If not, they replace the cards **in the same position**.
- The game continues until all the cards are used up. The winner is the student who finishes with the most pairs of matching cards.

5 Happy families

- Copy and cut up picture idioms, their corresponding written idioms and their definitions.
- Mix all the cards and shuffle.
- Deal half of them amongst the students.
- Put the remaining half face down on the table.
- Students look at their cards and try to make up as many 'families' of three (i.e., picture, idiom, definition), as possible.
- Students get rid of unwanted cards by putting them on the bottom of the spare cards pile and picking up a new card from the top of the pile.

6 Cloze

- Photocopy a selection of written idioms and blank out a key word (or several key words) from each of them.
- Students have to supply the missing word(s).

Groups: Divide the class into two teams. Write the missing words on the board. Read out the incomplete idiom – teams compete to provide the missing word. **Variation:** select one person from each team to come to the board. The teacher reads out the incomplete idiom, and the teams race against each other to circle the missing word on the board.

7 Guess the idiom

- Picture idioms are cut up and put in a bag.
- The teacher pulls out a card and holds it up for the student to see. The student has to guess the idiom.

Groups: Teams write down or shout out the answer.

Note: This activity can only be done once the students are familiar with the idioms.

8 Two-step bingo (groups)

- Divide picture idioms equally amongst students.
- Students place the cards face up in front of them.
- The teacher reads out an idiom at random.
- When a student hears one of his/her idioms read out, he/she turns over the relevant card.
- The first student to have all his idioms read out shouts 'bingo' and wins the game.

More challenging variation: Three-step bingo (groups)

The teacher can deal out the written idioms or definitions instead of the picture idioms.

9 Mime

A student takes one picture idiom from the pile and mimes what it depicts, while the other students guess what the idiom is.

10 Improvisation

- Cut up a selection of written idioms and put them in a bag.
- Two students (or a student and the teacher) each pick out one card from the bag and have to improvise a conversation using their idiom(s) correctly.
- As soon as they have used their idiom, another is picked from the bag.
- The winner is the person who has collected the most cards.

11 Relating idioms to real life

- Cut up a selection of written idioms and put them in a bag.
- A student picks out a card and has to talk about a real-life situation he/she has been in, incorporating that idiom into their story.

Variations:

a) Use picture idioms instead of written idioms.
b) Team game. Use definition cards. When the student tells his/her story using the definition, the opposite team has to decide which idiom it refers to.
c) True or false team game. Each person in the team has to tell a story which may or may not be true, using an idiom. The opposite team has to guess whether or not the story is true.
d) Chain story (groups). A student picks a card at random from a bag of picture or written idioms and uses it to start off a story or situation. The bag passes to the adjacent student who takes a card and has to continue the story using that idiom, and so on.

12 Anagrams

- Copy a page of written idioms.
- Blank out and reorder the letters of a key word (or several key words) from each idiom to make an anagram for the student to solve. (This would make a useful revision or homework activity.)

13 Make a million

- Put together four possible definitions – one true, three fictional – for a number of idioms.
- Read out an idiom and the four definitions.
- Starting with £100, a student has to identify the correct definition to double his/her money, in increments up to £1 million.

14 Snap

Note: this activity works best using two or three different pages of picture idioms

- Copy and cut up two sets of whichever picture idioms you want to use. Shuffle the cards and deal out equally between students.
- Without looking at the cards, students take turns to place a card face up on the table, as quickly as possible.
- If two identical cards are put face up consecutively, players must race to shout 'snap!' and **say the correct idiom**, in order to win the cards.
- The winner is the person with the most cards.

15 Pencil pictures (groups)

- Cut up a set of written idioms and place the cards face down near the front of the classroom.
- Divide the students into two teams.
- One student from each group looks at the top card, puts it face down and, from memory, has one minute to draw the idiom as quickly as possible, while their team tries to guess what the idiom is.
- The first team to guess correctly wins a point.
- The game continues with another student from each team taking turns to draw.

16 Three in a row

- Copy one set of definitions and use as a games board.
- Two students/teams take turns to choose a definition. If they can say the matching idiom, they win the square and it is crossed off.
- The aim of the game is to win as many rows of three pictures as possible – diagonally, horizontally or vertically.
- The game continues until no more moves are possible.

17 Right or wrong?

- Using a set of picture cards, one person picks a card at random and gives a definition.
- The other person has to decide whether the definition is right or wrong, and wins a point for each correct answer.
- Bonus points can be won (if necessary) if the correct definition is given.

18 Word chain (groups)

- Make up a card set of picture idioms – enough for one per student.
- Write the wrong idioms on the reverse and give each student a card.
- The teacher starts by reading out any one of the idioms and the student with that particular idiom has to turn over his card and read out his idiom to the class.
- The student with the matching idiom picture then reads out his/her idiom from the reverse of his card, and so on.

Note: This is also a great opportunity to correct pronunciation.

19 Hit on a headline

An opportunity for students to be creative!

- Cut out a variety of newspaper articles without their headlines.
- Students invent suitable headlines using as many idioms as possible from the section you are teaching.

Groups: Divide larger groups into teams and make this into a timed race; the team who has used the most captions wins.

20 Activities based on popular board games

Cut up picture idioms and use as question cards in board games such as Ludo or Taboo.

Part

B

Idiom summary

Bite the bullet: make yourself do or accept something difficult or unpleasant

Bend someone's ear: question someone in detail about something

Drag your heels: deal with something slowly, because you don't want to do it

A finger in every pie: be involved in or influence many different activities

Eat your words: admit that something you said was wrong

Hit the nail on the head: describe exactly what is causing a problem or situation

Draw a line under it: finish talking about a topic and not refer to it again

Make a mountain out of a molehill: make a minor difficulty seem like a major one

Keep your hair on: stay calm and patient

Put all your eggs in one basket: risk losing everything by limiting your options

Keep something under wraps: keep something secret or confidential

An uphill struggle: a difficult situation because something/someone is causing you problems

Ruffle someone's feathers: make someone angry or annoyed

Skate on thin ice: take a big risk

Bury your head in the sand: refuse to think about or deal with a situation

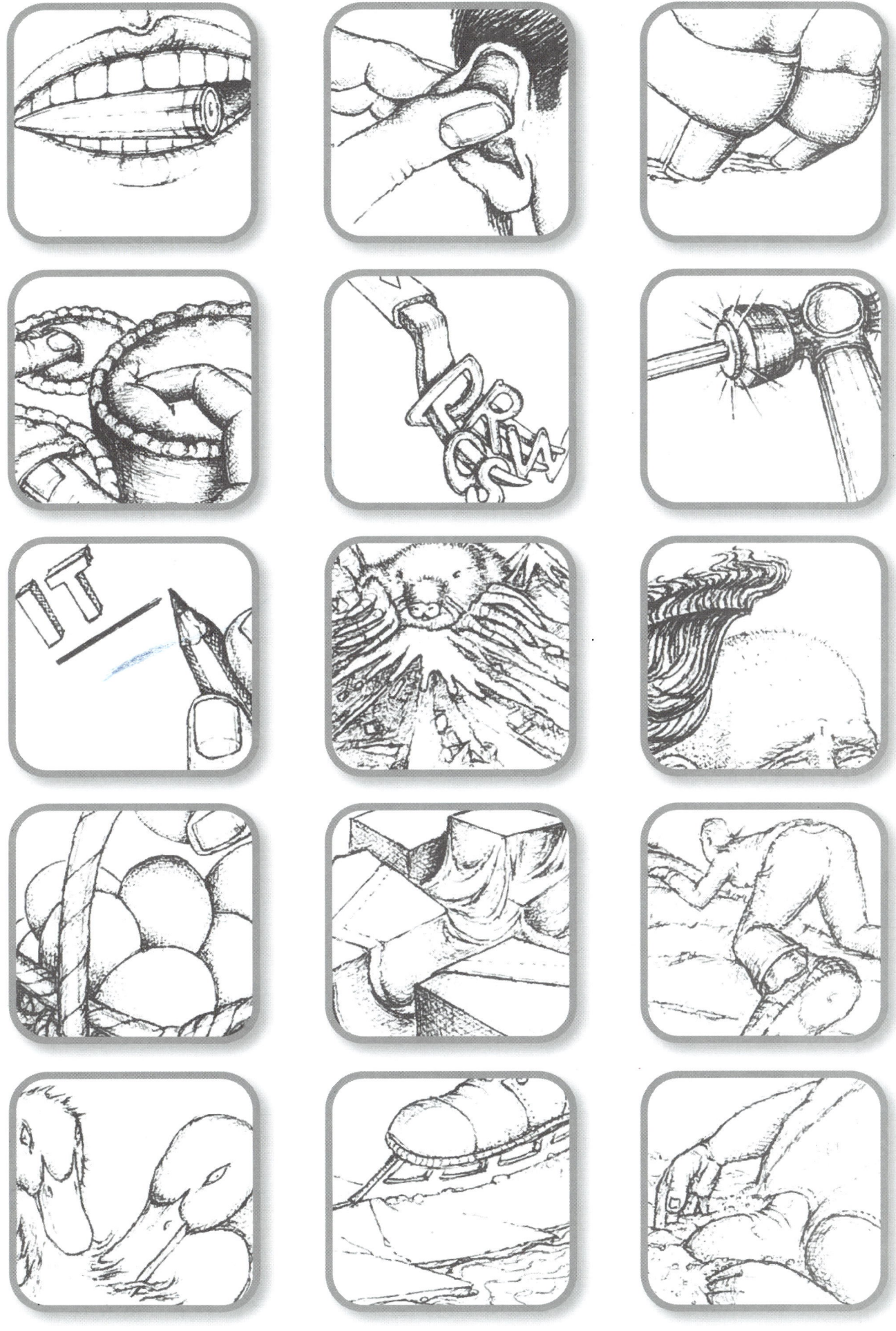

Drag your heels	Bend someone's ear	Bite the bullet
Hit the nail on the head	Eat your words	A finger in every pie
Keep your hair on	Make a mountain out of a molehill	Draw a line under it
An uphill struggle	Keep something under wraps	Put all your eggs in one basket
Bury your head in the sand	Skate on thin ice	Ruffle someone's feathers

make yourself do or accept something difficult or unpleasant

question someone in detail about something

deal with something slowly, because you don't want to do it

be involved in or influence many different activities

admit that something you said was wrong

describe exactly what is causing a problem or situation

finish talking about a topic and not refer to it again

make a minor difficulty seem like a major one

stay calm and patient

risk losing everything by limiting your options

keep something secret or confidential

a difficult situation because something/ someone is causing you problems

make someone angry or annoyed

take a big risk

refuse to think about or deal with a situation

Read all about it

Banks bite the bullet

The full disclosure requirement for banks to reveal their toxic assets continues to deal a severe blow to profits. Although unpopular with banks, the move was considered necessary to encourage more effective management of non-performing loans and to protect the shareholders.

Northern Gazeteer 24 November, 2008

Scientists attack government

The campaigns director of Eco-resolve Ltd **hit the nail on the head** when he stated that government spending was outrageous and unethical. A series of increasingly extravagant 'mini-summits' is squandering money which could instead be channelled into implementing effective environmental policies.

The Chronicler 14 April, 2008

Let's hear it for GM food

Far from damning genetically modified foods, let us stop being naïve in assuming that fresh, nutritious food is an option available to all. Millions of people rely on GM food for their survival. It's time to **eat our words** and accept that GM food is the only way that we can ensure enough food for the world population.

Wordsweek 20 June, 2009

Optimist or pessimist?

Ask five economists when they think the economic recovery will begin and you'll get five different answers. Unlike our government, which remains optimistic and which says critics of its economic policies during this recession are **making a mountain out of a molehill**.

Economics Daily 25 March, 2009

Has the apprenticeship scheme collapsed?

The apprenticeship scheme set up last year by the government has been one of the first victims of the recession, struggling along with a series of initiatives to keep the scheme going, mainly by getting apprentices to work on public projects. Industry leaders, union officials and apprentices themselves are understandably angry. But perhaps they would be well advised to **keep their hair on**, as the Government is about to announce a second set of initiatives next week which, they say, should improve the situation considerably.

Soapbox 1 May, 2009

Shareholding for beginners

Want to make a personal investment? It may be a laudable idea, but buying shares is a risky business for the uninitiated. Perhaps the most important piece of advice is don't **put all your eggs in one basket**. Investing your time, money and energy in a single endeavour can be a recipe for disaster in volatile financial markets. Instead, do as the professionals do and diversify your investments.

Wordsweek 13 January, 2009

Draw a line under Goodwin's past

The expression may be grim and closed to inquiry. But the face is instantly familiar. Sir Fred Goodwin, the deposed chief of Royal Bank of Scotland, is back in Edinburgh after a self-imposed exile abroad.

…this is a private return, made for his family and his children so that they can resume their education. The return should also mark the latest in a series of **lines** to be **drawn under** the events of the past year.

The Scotsman 17 August, 2009

Standard Life's new CEO under wraps

FOR years before Standard Life held its AGM in Edinburgh, the board would invite the business hacks round for dinner and a few drinks and a briefing from chief executive, Sir Sandy Crombie. But that was before the group announced Crombie was stepping down, opening wide the race for his successor. According to an SL spokeswoman the group is "having a very quiet AGM this year". Usually, there is some fire to fight – policy bonus cuts, secret equity sales, demutualisation – but the big question this time around is "who is it?"

The Scotsman 16 May, 2009

Finding that job

For those of us who cannot rely on inheriting the family business, looking for a job is a harsh reality. But with fierce competition, what can you do to gain an advantage in the jobs market? One of the best tips is to **bend the ears** of careers advice professionals. Career advisers usually go to exceptional lengths to help people, especially when jobs are in short supply, and they hold databases of useful contacts which the average job hunter would never be able to access.

Daily Recorder 3 June, 2009

Consumers cash in on bank charges test case

Britain's biggest banks have been ordered to refund unauthorised overdraft charges to their customers. A landmark test case in the High Court ruled that excessive bank charges were unjustifiable. It remains to be seen whether the banks will now refund their customers promptly, or **drag their heels** by going to the court of appeal.

Business Bugle 1 August, 2009

Challenging times ahead for property developers

Many of the UK's housebuilders, including several household names, face **an uphill struggle** as property prices sink. Many would-be first time buyers have been biding their time in the private rental sector, ready to pounce once the outlook improves. One of the main reasons for the slowdown is mortgage deposit rates, which now average 25% and are set to remain high for the foreseeable future

Northern Weekly Chronicle 7 February, 2009

Don't be afraid to ruffle feathers

The trouble with the English is that we're too polite. We often attribute sloppy work and/or missed deadlines to a variety of unlikely excuses, and even managers prefer to give employees the benefit of the doubt rather than discipline them. But to be a successful troubleshooter you often need to **ruffle** a few **feathers**, otherwise seemingly insignificant problems can escalate quickly into more serious ones.

Soapbox 28 August, 2009

CEOs 'skating on thin ice'

The performance of many of our leaders of industry is coming under heavy scrutiny in these difficult times. On average, industry profits are estimated to have slipped by 25-36%, leaving many Chief Executive Officers (CEOs) wondering what they will say to their shareholders at the next AGM and, more importantly for them, how they will fare in the dwindling jobs market.

Daily Recorder 24 October, 2008

Celebrity support

You may think you are powerless to prevent high rise, high density housing opposite your carefully tended front garden, but there is a solution. Instead of **burying your head in the sand**, why not approach an A-list celebrity to champion your cause? This approach is becoming increasingly popular, as the publicity it generates tends to result in a high success rate. Local authorities, however, are anxious to dispel this as a myth, usually citing other reasons for their backing down.

People's Courier 2 March, 2009

A finger in every pie

Government control extends far beyond the nationalised banks. Thanks to the credit crunch, it is now intervening in economic activity on an unprecedented scale – curbing City bonuses, introducing a scrappage scheme for old cars to kick-start the motor industry, and so on. Whatever business sector you care to name, the government is bound to have had its **fingers in the** corporate **pie**.

Business Bugle 2 May, 2009

Exercises

1 Combine the words in the box to make five idioms. Use each word only once.

your	put	words	eggs	on	heels	thin
every	basket	eat	in	a	skating	pie	your
your	one	all	in	finger	drag	ice

_____

_____

_____

_____

_____

2 Now put the idioms from Exercise 1 into the sentences below. You may have to change the possessive pronoun.

a) If you want to know what's going on, ask Dave. He has _____.

b) You thought the figures were correct, but you were wrong. You'll have to _____.

c) If you _____ for too long, you'll lose the sale.

d) I think we should take a risk, even though we'll be _____.

e) When you are investing money, it's better not to _____

_____.

3 Discussion.

a) Talk about some situations in which you have had to bite the bullet.

b) Give an example of a situation in which an employee might want to bend their boss's ear.

c) If you hit the nail on the head, is it a positive or negative situation?

d) Have you ever had to keep a business decision under wraps?

e) Find two idioms in this section which can have the opposite meaning.

f) Do you know anyone who makes a mountain out of a molehill? Is there an idiom for this in your language?

g) Some people love to ruffle feathers. How easy is it to ruffle _your_ feathers?

h) If someone is taking their time over doing a job, what could you say to them?

4 Choose the correct meaning of a–d.

a) If you *bury your head in the sand* you are:
   i) avoiding an issue ❑   ii) working too hard ❑   iii) concealing mistakes ❑

b) If you find something is *an uphill struggle*, is it:
   i) quite difficult ❑   ii) very difficult ❑   iii) impossible ❑

c) If you *keep your hair on*, you are:
   i) keeping a secret ❑   ii) keeping calm ❑   iii) delaying something ❑

d) *Drawing a line under it* is:
   i) emphasizing how important it is ❑   ii) disagreeing ❑
   iii) to finish discussing something ❑

e) *Making a mountain out of a molehill* is:
   i) improving a situation ❑   ii) taking a risk ❑
   iii) making a small problem seem bigger ❑

5 In the dialogue, replace the more formal phrases in bold with a suitable idiom:

A: It's no good **delaying our decision** any longer, we need to **go ahead** and redesign the spreadsheets.

_____

B: Well, it's going to **upset a few people**, especially our boss. He wanted to **keep the idea secret** for a bit longer.

_____

A: Keeping anything secret in our organization is **a difficult task** – but **avoiding the issue** is crazy!

_____

B: OK Mike, **stay calm**! I'll **talk to** the boss. Although it seems like we're **taking a big risk,** if I can explain why we need to implement the changes quickly, I'm sure he'll give us the go-ahead and then we can **finish discussing it** and move on to the next project.

_____

Bite the bullet

In the days before effective anaesthetics, soldiers were given bullets to bite on to help them endure pain.

Idiom summary

Sweep something under the carpet: hide a problem in the hope that it will be forgotten

Bang your head against a brick wall: keep trying to solve a problem and being unsuccessful

Have a bee in your bonnet: preoccupied or obsessed with a particular idea

Bend over backwards: make a special effort to do something

Dig your heels in: be stubborn/refuse to give in

Back to square one: start again from the beginning

A card up your sleeve: have a reserve plan or secret advantage

Water under the bridge: past event which is no longer worth considering

Get to grips with something: start to deal with a difficult job or situation

A spanner in the works: prevent something being achieved

In the hot seat: be the focus of attention

A piece of cake: something easily achieved

Break the ice: help people feel more relaxed with each other

Get your wires crossed: misunderstand something

On the tip of your tongue: almost but not quite able to remember something

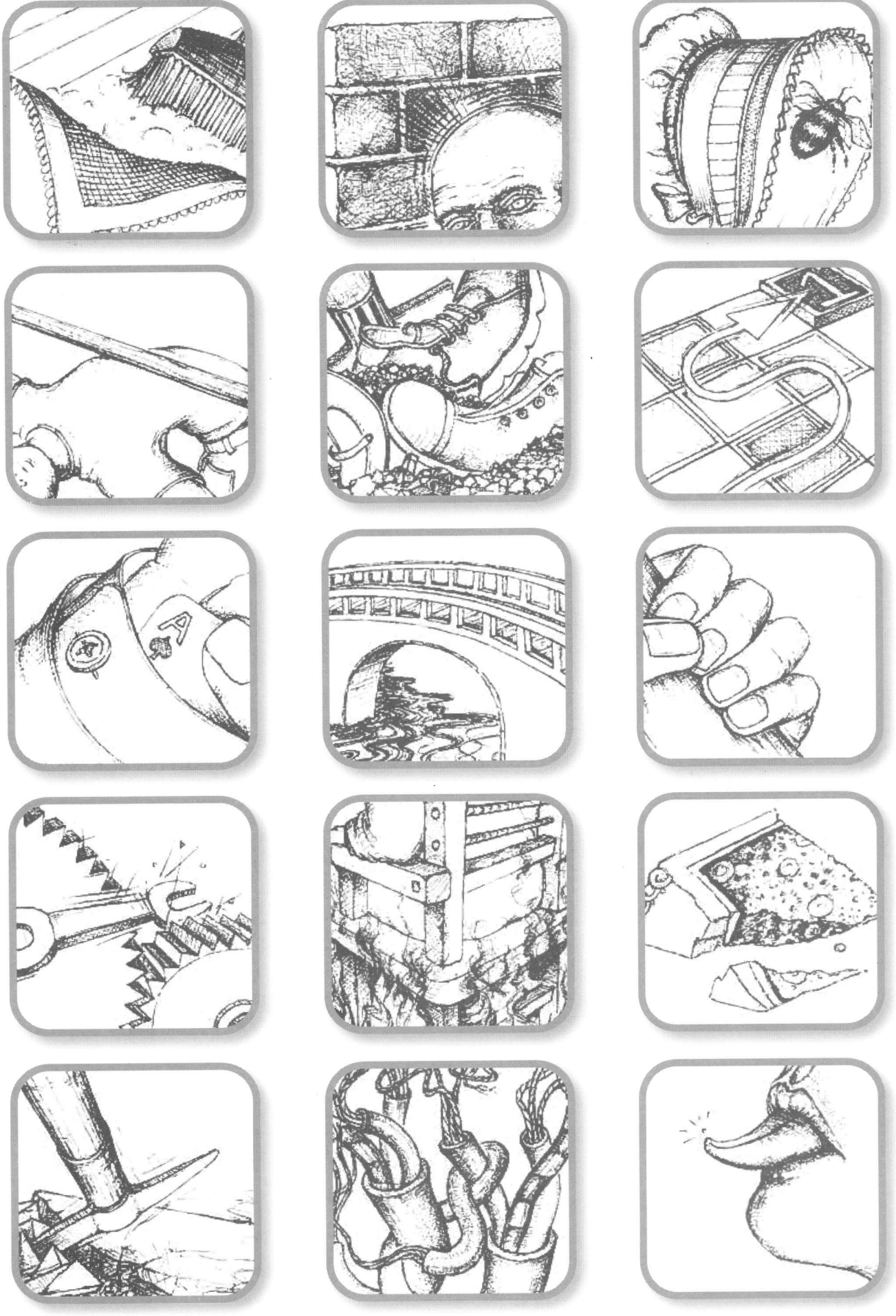

Have a bee in your bonnet	Bang your head against a brick wall	Sweep something under the carpet
Back to square one	Dig your heels in	Bend over backwards
Get to grips with something	Water under the bridge	A card up your sleeve
A piece of cake	In the hot seat	A spanner in the works
On the tip of your tongue	Get your wires crossed	Break the ice

hide a problem in the hope that it will be forgotten	keep trying to solve a problem and being unsuccessful	preoccupied or obsessed with a particular idea
make a special effort to do something	be stubborn/ refuse to give in	start again from the beginning
have a reserve plan or secret advantage	past event which is no longer worth considering	start to deal with a difficult job or situation
prevent something from being achieved	be the focus of attention	something easily achieved
help people feel more relaxed with each other	misunderstand something	almost but not quite able to remember something

Read all about it

Oops! It's opera

A company director from Kent was stopped by police last week for playing a Mozart opera 'too loudly'.

Mr Sands said: "It went from ludicrous to unbelievable. The police officer definitely had **a bee in his bonnet** about something.
I even had the car windows closed."

"In the end he reluctantly admitted that I hadn't committed an offence, but still took a note of all my details. Personally, I just think he was just bored and decided to stop me for something to do."

People's Courier 15 May, 2009

Time to speed up switching

Want a better broadband deal? Changing your service provider is not as easy as you may think. Many customers find it complicated comparing 'like for like' deals, To make matters worse, once they have chosen to change, if the service request is not correctly logged for any reason, they can end up **back at square one**. Too many people report having no service at all for anything up to two weeks, especially if they are classed as a 'domestic' user, as opposed to a 'business' one.

Wordsweek 12 January, 2009

Rift over

The well-publicised hostilities between the Deery twins are over at last. The rift between the successful investment banking duo is rumoured to have started over a relatively trivial matter, escalating to a point where the two would not attend the same functions as each other – something very difficult to sustain in the close-knit London banking scene. Common sense, however, prevailed, when a mutual friend acted as intermediary. "**Water goes under the bridge** quite quickly in the banking world," a colleague commented.

Business Bugle 24 May, 2008

Councils 'dig their heels in'

Despite the public outcry over yet another council tax increase – the second this year – local councils are **digging their heels in** and insisting that the increases are necessary to cover bigger overheads such as rising fuel costs. "We're being conned", said pensioner Fred Blakeney, "our rubbish bins are now only emptied once every two weeks, instead of weekly, yet councillors in our area have just accepted a 6% pay rise. We're not getting value for money."

Daily Discoverer 20 July, 2009

Motivating your staff

Trying to motivate and keep good, experienced staff can be a perennial problem, and you may feel like you are **banging your head against a brick wall**. But try to follow these simple rules and you may be pleasantly surprised:

- Listen to what your staff tell you. A comparatively small problem can escalate into a more serious one if not dealt with promptly, and could result in your employees scouring the jobs pages in the local newspaper. If there is a good reason why you can't take action to sort out a problem, tell them why.
- Make a habit of regularly getting involved with daily tasks. Your staff will see that you are interested and approachable.
- Give feedback whenever you can. Don't leave it until the annual review – compliment anyone who has put in extra effort, for example, to meet a deadline. And how about taking them out for a drink sometime? You'll be surprised how much you learn about your business when having an informal chat!
- Set clear work objectives and career paths. You can lose good staff just because they don't realise you have great plans for their future in the company. Show them that you value them.
- Team building. When recruiting, try to choose people who you feel will fit in with your existing staff. This doesn't always work, but it gets you off to a good start. And try organising a teambuilding activity, such as sailing or paintballing, from time to time.

Business Bugle 12 November, 2008

Environmental criticism unjustified, say airlines

According to the Intergovernmental Panel on Climate Change (IPCC), pollution from the aviation industry accounts for only 2% of global greenhouse gas emissions, a view which is supported by airlines. However, the media gives the impression that environmental damage from this industry is double that amount. The major carriers continue to refute this, although many critics think that they are trying to **sweep** the true figures **under the carpet**.

National Grapevine 23 December, 2008

Simplify the small print

It's happened to all of us. You sign up for a seemingly lucrative savings account, only to find that there are a host of little surcharges, penalty fees and other restrictions which were not drawn to your attention at the time of opening the account. Of course, the banks are covered – 'you should have read the small print!' they declare smugly. However, it is very annoying that they never seem to **bend over backwards** to simplify things for the customer.

Business Break 21 August, 2009

How baking can help children earn a crust

"You can't bake cakes without maths," says the Minister for Adult Education. Mathematical competence is really important to employment success, and the government is hoping to inspire adults who lack mathematical skills by subsidising cookery classes for them. So far the response has been encouraging. "I hated Maths at school", said one woman we interviewed, "but cooking is a favourite hobby of mine, and I don't want to ruin recipes because I've weighed the ingredients wrongly. I think this incentive is an ideal way to **get to grips with** maths."

Daily Focus 28 January, 2009

Getting back in the black

A record number of British householders now have three or more credit cards, and many of those people are regularly spending up to their limit every month. The problems arise because there is a temptation to pay off the minimum amount each month, so that interest charges spiral out of control. The **spanner in the works**, say the economists, has been the availability of instant credit and the fistfuls of store credit cards that have been issued too readily.

Daily Focus 22 February, 2008

Chairman in the hot seat

Lord Michaels, veteran of leading accountancy giant BFDP, has presided over two profit warnings, with the potential collapse of the global economy still to come. He has been chairman of the company for only eight months, and probably knew it was never going to be easy. "It's been quite an interesting period," he said, with typical understatement.

Economics Daily 19 June, 2009

Rebranding a 'piece of cake' for local retailer

When Normans, the Suffolk bakery chain, decided on a total rebrand of its 15 outlets, they instantly approached Suffolk Signwriters. The brief was outlined by the client, several options were mocked up, and samples manufactured and submitted for approval. Once the decision by Normans had been made and the order received, production began immediately due to the very tight deadline set by the client. The whole project was completed without any setbacks and the customer is delighted. Suffolk Signwriters said that they were a long-established company with an experienced team of workers, and as a result the whole process went smoothly and to plan.

Northern Reporter 11 December, 2008

ARC Enterprises

There are no **crossed wires** in our organisation. In a questionnaire, 86% say communication/ reporting lines are clear. 77% know who does what in the firm. 87% say meetings are well prepared, relevant and effective. 72% of employees feel valued and receive recognition for their efforts, and 85% of staff are proud to work for us.

HR Post 28 May, 2008

Cultural Quirks

Doing business in a foreign country can be a daunting experience, not least because of the cultural differences that, if not respected, can make or break a deal. So, what advice could be given to someone who wants to **break the ice** at a business meeting in the UK? Well you could try the old favourite – comment on the weather. In my experience, it never fails to get an enthusiastic vocal response.

Wordsweek 22 August, 2008

Employees beware!

In a recession-streaked 2009, even the most conscientious workers have resorted to a new approach to the work-life balance: telling lies, lazing around and leaving work early. But the risks can be considerable. If you must resort to taking time out from your stressful job, make sure you have a plausible excuse **on the tip of your tongue**.

Business Bugle 31 April, 2009

Starting afresh

Sandra Shaw lost her job earlier this year. But far from being devastated, she has a **card up her sleeve** in the form of a five-figure redundancy payment from her company. She has a number of ideas to make her money work harder. One way would be to use part of it as a deposit on a buy-to-let property. Another option is to put her money into savings and investments. And a third and favourite option, she is considering starting her own company. "It's risky, but I have a lot of experience behind me and I'm not afraid of hard work. This is a once-in-a-lifetime opportunity for me, and I think working for myself will be refreshing and rewarding."

Business Break 10 November, 2008

Exercises

1 **Complete the idioms in the sentences with the correct preposition.**

a) We're trying to sort out the problem, but it's like banging our heads _____ a brick wall.

b) The hotel staff bent _____ backwards to make my stay comfortable.

c) Never relax when you're negotiating with Dan, he always has a card _____ his sleeve.

d) Dig your heels _____ when they ask for better terms, this is the best discount we can offer.

2 **Unscramble the key words in the box, and use them to complete the idioms.**

ISWER	CKAE	ERKAB	GRSUGETL

a) I started talking to the visitors in an effort to _____ the ice.

b) I thought the exam would be difficult, but it was a piece of _____!

c) The meeting is tomorrow, not today – you must have got your _____ crossed.

d) This negotiation is going to be an uphill _____.

3 **In each conversation, the second speaker (B) agrees with what the first speaker (A) says. Complete the sentences with the correct idiom.**

i) **A:** The strike certainly caused problems on the production line, didn't it?

   B: Yes, it really put _____.

ii) **A:** I think you'll be the focus of attention in this afternoon's meeting.

   B: Yes, I expect I'll be _____!

iii) **A:** Let's scrap this idea and start again.

   B: I agree. We have to go _____.

4 Discussion.

a) When you have problems at work, do you get to grips with them or sweep them under the carpet? Which of these does a *procrastinator* do?

b) Have you ever had a bee in your bonnet about something? Give an example.

c) What could you say if you are having difficulty remembering a word? Does this happen more frequently when you speak English, or when you are speaking in your own language?

d) Talk about some idioms in your own language that may be similar to those in this section. Can any of the idioms be translated word for word?

5 Complete the crossword. Each of the clues are definitions of idioms. Choose *one* word from each correct idiom to complete the crossword.

Across

1 When you keep trying to solve a problem without success (noun).

4 You can become obsessed with something so that you can't think about anything else (noun).

5 You can almost, but not quite, remember something (noun).

Down

1 Sometimes a past event is no longer important (noun).

2 Some people do this to hide a problem (noun).

3 Preventing something from being achieved (noun).

Back to square one

The children's playground game *hopscotch* is played on a grid of numbered squares on the ground. Usually, it involves players throwing a stone onto a consecutively higher number, then hopping from square to square, missing out the square containing their thrown stone. They go from one to (usually) ten, and then back to square one.

Idiom summary

A chip on your shoulder: be resentful about a past experience

Full of hot air: saying things which are not valuable or useful

Take the bull by the horns: deal decisively with a difficult situation

Pick holes: find fault with or blame someone

Sit on the fence: avoid making a choice or decision

Pay through the nose: pay more than the fair price

Splitting hairs: making small, unnecessary distinctions

Get/start the ball rolling: get something started

Read between the lines: look for a hidden or implied meaning

Left holding the baby: be left with an unwelcome responsibility

Jump the gun: act before the correct time

Put something on the back-burner: make something a low priority

Over the top (OTT): do more than is necessary or appropriate

At the eleventh hour: at the latest possible moment

Down in the mouth: be or look unhappy

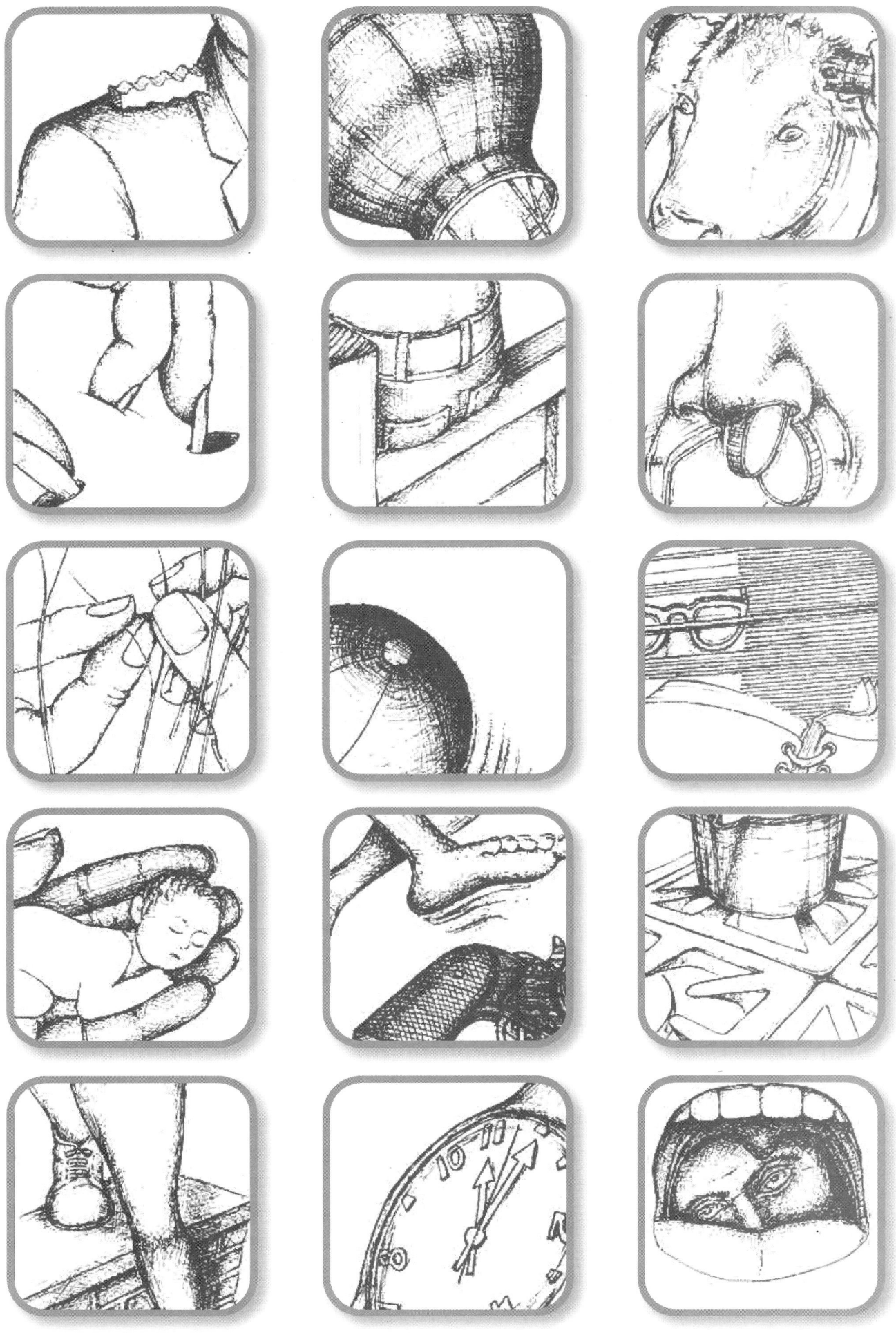

Take the bull by the horns	Full of hot air	A chip on your shoulder
Pay through the nose	Sit on the fence	Pick holes
Read between the lines	Get/start the ball rolling	Splitting hairs
Put something on the back-burner	Jump the gun	Left holding the baby
Down in the mouth	At the eleventh hour	Over the top (OTT)

be resentful about a past experience	saying things which are not valuable or useful	deal decisively with a difficult situation
find fault with or blame someone	avoid making a choice or decision	pay more than the fair price
making small, unnecessary distinctions	get something started	look for a hidden or implied meaning
be left with an unwelcome responsibility	act before the correct time	make something a low priority
do more than is necessary or appropriate	at the latest possible moment	be or look unhappy

Read all about it

American angst

The common impression of Americans is that they are confident, successful and maybe just a little bit brash. Not so, argues a leading US psychologist. She maintains that a lot of her contemporaries have an inferiority complex regarding the British. "A lot of Americans have **a chip on their shoulder**. They think the British regard themselves as being a more cultured and sophisticated race which looks down on Americans and their way of life. However, I have spent many years in the UK and have discovered the British, if a little reserved at first, are a generous, friendly and tolerant nation."

Soapbox 2 August, 2009

Criticism of crisis handling

Leaders of the two main opposition parties yesterday accused the Prime Minister of failing to handle the financial crisis promptly and effectively. A spokesman for the Liberal Union party said "Everyone thinks this government is **full of hot air** and is incapable of leading our country out of one of the biggest financial crises in history."

Weekly Informer 12 November, 2008

Car industry woes

Motor manufacturers yesterday announced that orders are down by 30 per cent. Production cuts in the global car industry are accelerating at an alarming rate, with another five thousand job losses announced this week, bringing the total to 15,000 worldwide. But the companies who are **taking the bull by the horns** and cutting unnecessary overheads now, rather than wait until they're forced to, are likely to recover more quickly as the recession comes to an end.

Northern Reporter 3 November, 2008

A new perspective on education

In a week of gloomy comments about falling educational standards, an announcement by the Department of Education may provide a glimmer of optimism…. There are two ways of looking at this story. The first is to welcome their proposed end to continuous testing in schools, and the stress it puts pupils under. The second is to **pick holes** in it, and regard it as another misguided decision which will cost the taxpayer yet more money.

Soapbox 9 March, 2009

Market view 2009

While most house values crashed by a fifth last year, homes in popular areas fell by just 15%. Estate agents say many potential buyers walked out of the market in the second half of the year because of the credit crunch and negative publicity. They hope credit will become more readily available in the second half of 2009, tempting those who are currently **sitting on the fence** to come back into the market.

Data Daily 2 January, 2009

Closing time for the British pub?

Ten per cent of the 57,000 pubs in England and Wales are predicted to close over the next five years. Pub landlords blame the culture of stay-at-home drinking because of cheap booze sold in supermarkets; the credit crunch forcing people to keep a closer eye on their expenditure; the smoking ban; and limitations placed on tenant landlords by the breweries. The latter, known as "the tie", has come under attack because it forces landlords to **pay through the nose** for rent and beer, making their pubs uncompetitive.

Daily Discoverer 10 March, 2009

No longer splitting hairs over splitting atoms?

As public opinion shifts and many more governments around the world consider nuclear energy as a solution to climate concerns and energy security, it is time to examine why it has become a more attractive option.

If the nuclear plants currently generating electricity in Europe were shut down and replaced with fossil fuel-derived power plants, 700 million more tonnes of carbon dioxide would be emitted each year, equivalent to doubling the number of cars on European roads.

Although there are greenhouse gas emissions associated with the mining, enrichment and fuel fabrication of uranium, and the construction of nuclear power plants, they are very small in comparison with the emissions of stations burning fossil fuels, and comparable with the emissions from renewable electricity sources like wind, wave and solar.

As Adrian Bull, UK stakeholder manager for Westinghouse, a global nuclear company, said … "Comparing the greenhouse gas emissions of nuclear power plants with those from renewables is like comparing the calorie content of cucumbers and lettuces."

ESOF seminar 2008

Let's get the ball rolling

The biggest story in the financial news this week is that the government has officially delayed appointing a commissioner of financial advisers who will implement new rules around the taxation of life insurance products. They insist the changes will happen eventually – but now is really time to **get the ball rolling**.

Weekly Informer 13 May, 2009

The best MBAs – read between the lines

Managers choose to study for an MBA to get a better job. But before you choose the institution where you want to study, do some careful research. League tables are misleading, as they are based on who has most research published in academic journals. This is no guarantee that the courses run by these institutions will be suitable for you. Visit the college, ask searching questions and, if possible, seek personal recommendations.

Economics Daily 19 July, 2009

Financial babysitting

Property companies and mortgage borrowers are defaulting in rapidly rising numbers as the property slump takes effect, leaving the banks that financed them **holding the baby**. Defaults and repossessions are turning banks into some of the country's biggest estate agents.

People's Courier 22 January, 2009

Looking ahead

The features and dimensions of the next versions of the iPod touch and iPod Nano are China's worst-kept secret. So much so that manufacturers in China have already started producing cases for the devices. A case of **jumping the gun**, perhaps? The revised iPod models are due in September this year.

People's Courier 30 July, 2009

Eleventh hour intervention saves historic printing company

Almost 40 jobs have been cut at the printing division of The People's Printer, one of the oldest printing companies in the world. However, after a concerted effort by existing customers and academic authors, the company's management bowed to pressure and agreed to retain the remaining staff.

Northern Reporter 27 March, 2009

High expectations for new leader

Every newly-elected leader of a country faces a demanding transition period, but even more so at a time where the recession is deepening; the banks, car industry and housing market are in a state of meltdown; and the budget deficit is going sky high.

None of these problems can be solved instantly, but the electors will expect their leader to prioritise, putting some issues **on the back-burner** and leaving others in the hands of senior politicians.

Soapbox 11 August, 2009

Cheer up; you have alternatives

Not got the exam grades you need for your university of choice? There's no reason to be **down in the mouth**, says Professor Steven Duke, of the University of the Southern Counties. Your first option is to contact the clearing house, who may be able to offer a place for the same or a similar subject at another university. You might also consider resitting one or more of your exams, or redoing them completely over one year. If none of these options appeals, some companies will employ you and subsidise your studies at night school. And if all else fails, take a gap year and do some community service overseas. You may return with totally different ideas of what you want to do with your life!

The Daily Focus 20 August, 2009

Go over the top to connect with wealthy clients

The days of big spending are over for many, but the really affluent just need a little encouragement to continue spending. Lavish parties and extravagant events are in vogue as the economic slowdown forces companies to woo their high-net-worth customers. The message to businesses is: make extra efforts to appeal to the financially advantaged.

Business Break 14 December,

Exercises

1 Fill in the missing words in these sentences.

a) You look a bit down in the _____ Keith. What's the problem?
Well, everyone's gone to lunch and I've been left _____ the _____!

b) Why do you leave everything to the eleventh _____? You should take the
_____ by the _____ and prepare the figures before the deadline.

c) Right, everyone, welcome to the meeting. Mary, will you get the _____
_____ for us please?

d) We don't have to submit these figures until the end of the month. Let's put them on the
_____.

2 Choose an idiom which can replace the bold words, using the keyword given in brackets.

a) I think if we accept their proposal now, we'll be **acting too soon**. Let's wait and see if they come
up with a better offer. (GUN) _____

b) To be honest, I don't listen much to what Frank says. He's always **talking about unimportant
things**. (AIR) _____

c) Jane says she's leaving her job because it's boring. But **I think the real reason** is that she's been
told to leave because her work is below standard. (LINES)

_____

d) Let's stick to important matters, instead of **discussing minor details**. (HAIRS)

_____

e) Don't **make too much effort** to impress the Chairman. He's spending only a few minutes in this
department. (TOP) _____

Put the words in the correct order to make sentences.

a) have / because / shoulder / you / promotion / a / get / on / chip / your / didn't / you / do / that?

_____

_____

b) he / work / really / picks / I / my / boss / – / in / always / dislike / holes / my.

_____

_____

c) mobile / I've / the / contract / nose / my / paid / for / phone / through.

_____

_____

d) the / Dave / decision / prefers / on / making / a / instead / to / fence / of / sit.

_____

_____

4 **Discussion.**

a) Have you ever paid through the nose for something?

b) What sort of things do you leave to the eleventh hour? Why?

c) If you are feeling down in the mouth, what cheers you up?

d) You are at a meeting which is running late. This is because Jim, the human resources manager, is always full of hot air. Liz has a chip on her shoulder because she hasn't had a chance to speak. Sue is picking holes in everybody's suggestions and Bill won't make any decisions – he prefers to sit on the fence. What could you say to each of your colleagues to ensure the meeting doesn't overrun?

A chip on your shoulder

In the 18th century, dock workers in the Royal Navy dockyards were allowed to keep unwanted wood (chips) for building materials and firewood. They usually carried this away on their shoulders. However, a later ruling stated that only wood which could be carried under one arm could be removed. The dockers were very unhappy; they ignored the order and continued to carry 'chips on their shoulders'.

Idiom summary

Stick your neck out: give an opinion which may not be popular

Throw the baby out with the bathwater: get rid of good as well as bad parts of something

Bite someone's head off: react angrily to someone

Open a can of worms: reveal something which will cause trouble or embarrassment

A big fish in a small pond: a person seen as important, but within a small environment

A hard nut to crack: a difficult problem to solve

Iron/smooth something out: resolve minor difficulties

The wrong end of the stick: misunderstand a situation

Have a bone to pick: discuss something which has annoyed you

Put the cart before the horse: have your priorities the wrong way round

Spill the beans: reveal a secret or the truth about something

Cut corners: do things the easiest, quickest or cheapest way

Draw the line: put a limit on something because you think it is wrong

Play/keep your cards close to your chest: not tell anyone what your plans are

Nail/pin someone down: make another person deal with an issue

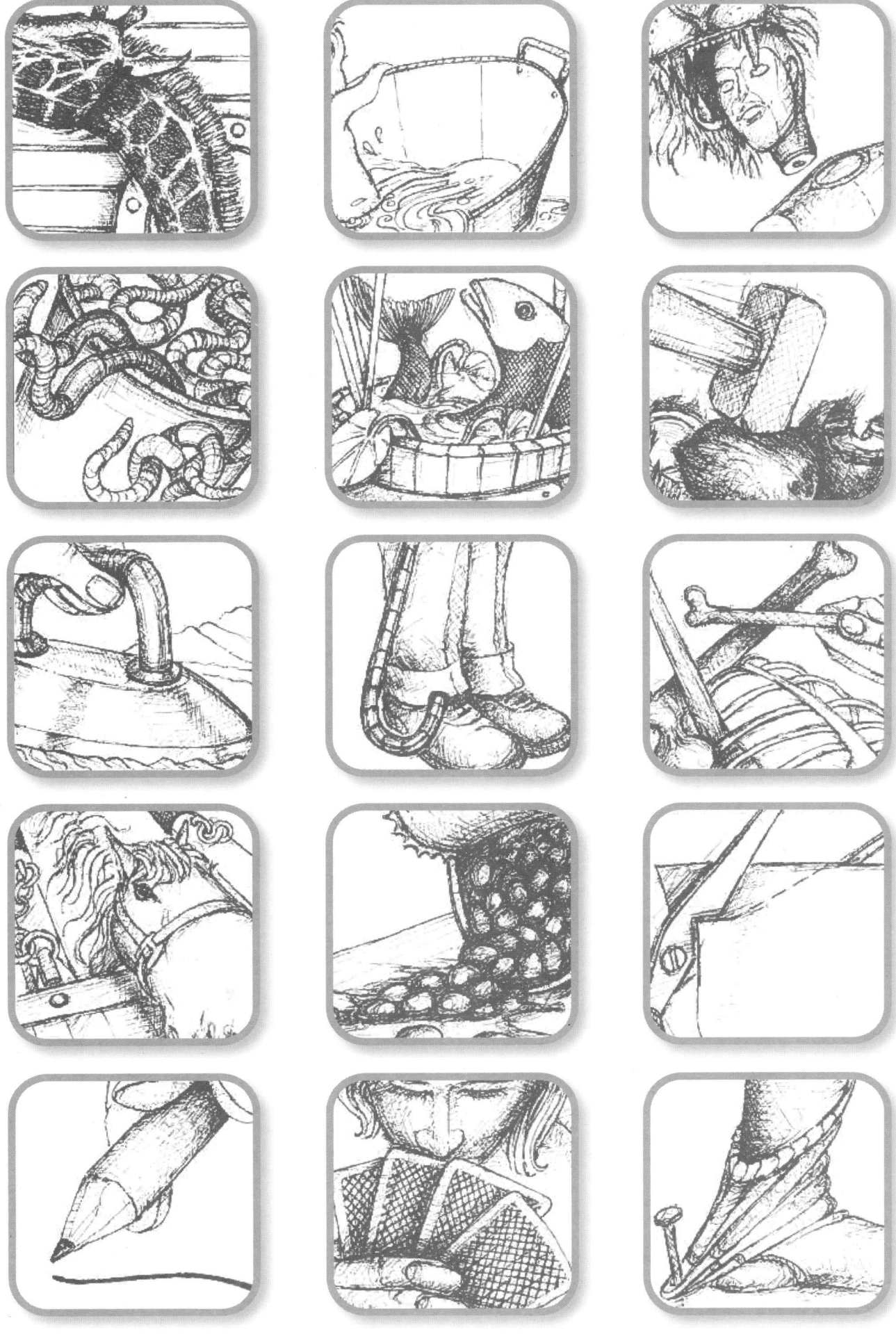

Bite someone's head off	Throw the baby out with the bathwater	Stick your neck out
A hard nut to crack	A big fish in a small pond	Open a can of worms
Have a bone to pick	The wrong end of the stick	Iron/smooth something out
Cut corners	Spill the beans	Put the cart before the horse
Nail/pin someone down	Play/keep your cards close to your chest	Draw the line

give an opinion which may not be popular

get rid of good as well as bad parts of something

react angrily to someone

reveal something which will cause trouble or embarrassment

a person seen as important, but within a small environment

a difficult problem to solve

resolve minor difficulties

misunderstand a situation

discuss something which has annoyed you

have your priorities the wrong way round

reveal a secret or the truth about something

do things the easiest, quickest or cheapest way

put a limit on something because you think it is wrong

not tell anyone what your plans are

make another person deal with an issue

Read all about it

Middle East airlines top the charts

Having recently flown on half a dozen Middle Eastern airlines in as many months, the difference between these and other major air carriers is striking. I have been more than impressed by the courtesy of the staff, the standard of the aircraft, the quality of the food, and the ease of check-in. I am prepared to **stick my neck out** and make a prediction: when we come out of the current credit crunch, these airlines will have become the leading lights in international aviation.

Soapbox 6 January, 2009

New educational guidelines for school teachers

At the moment, many teachers are under pressure to stick solely to the national curriculum.

The Department of Education has now set out new guidelines whereby teachers will no longer have to stick solely to textbooks but will be free to use their imagination. Brighter students will be fast-tracked and the slower students will be taught at their own pace, so teachers won't have to set classroom standards to the lowest common denominator.

But while the powers that be hope the guidelines will improve the quality of teaching and learning in schools, some teachers reckon they have **the wrong end of the stick**. They say that without a simultaneous review of everything – from syllabuses to teaching to examinations – teachers and students will remain trapped in a vicious circle.

National Echo 19 February, 2009

Help with mortgage arrears

If you are having difficulty paying your mortgage – maybe you have lost your job, a new baby has arrived, household bills are putting pressure on your finances - don't panic!

The first thing to bear in mind is that lenders have procedures for helping people who are experiencing payment difficulties. The next thing to do is contact your lender – they won't **bite your head off**, as they are obliged by regulation to treat you fairly and take into account your circumstances. Your mortgage company may be able to structure a payment plan to help you through your difficulties. This could involve:
- reducing your monthly payments for a specified time
- allowing you to change to an interest only mortgage
- giving you a payment 'holiday' or
- extending the term of your mortgage, thereby reducing your monthly payments.

Daily Recorder 23 September, 2008

Buyers beware?

Investors could be forgiven for wishing that they had never heard of building society Southern Reach. Nobody had any idea how big **a can of worms** its financial problems were. Now, with a government bailout, the company appears to be back on track – but for the average man in the street it is a matter of 'once bitten, twice shy'.

Wordsweek 22 March, 2009

Sink or swim

There's a general belief that it's best to be a **big fish in a small pond**. You have an opportunity to display your strengths and develop skills which may be impossible in a bigger corporate environment. However, those with outstanding merits rise to the challenge of greater competition and become even bigger fish when transferred to a big pond.

Business Break 21 June, 2008

For Barclays, retail biz a hard nut to crack in India

More and more foreign banks are discovering that doing business in the Indian retail loan market is akin to skating on thin ice. In 2002, French bank BNP Paribas shut down its retail banking operations. Over the past year, both Citi and HSBC have been hit by mounting losses in their retail and consumer finance portfolios. The latest casualty is Barclays, which is trying to shift focus from lower-end mass market for personal loans and consumer finance to higher-end personal loans and secured assets to contain mounting losses. "In India, impairments on retail portfolios have risen, as referenced in Barclays Group's 1Q09 interim management statement (IMS). This is due to the economic slowdown, which is putting pressure on our customers, and to some degree, the maturation of these portfolios," said Mark Jones, regional MD – Asia Barclays global retail and commercial business (GRCB). "Increased impairments are to be expected in this environment, but the important point is how you manage them... We have strengthened our collections processes and tightened our lending criteria on new applications," he said.

The Economic Times
19 June, 2009
© Bennett, Coleman & Co. Ltd.
All Rights Reserved

The effective employee

If you have **a bone to pick with** your boss, what is the best way of dealing with it? You could always drop hints, a typically English, indirect way of approaching sensitive issues. The risk is that the signals may be too subtle to be picked up on, or that what you are saying is not taken seriously enough. The other end of the scale is to deal with the problem directly and immediately. This may be more stressful, but is more likely to be effective. The downside is that you may be regarded as a troublemaker. And lastly, if it's a sufficiently important issue, raise it at the weekly departmental meeting. Don't forget to check out the opinion of your fellow workers beforehand, though!

Business Break 18 October, 2008

Time to take action on business malpractice

In recent months, we have witnessed many dishonest types of business behaviour, not least in our own government with the revelations relating to inflated ministerial expenses claims.

Seeing wealthy people walking away with millions of pounds while ordinary citizens bear the brunt of the economic collapse has been a catalyst for frustration and anger among those who will now see their incomes adversely affected by an inevitable rise in taxation or unemployment.

Why have those who actually acted dishonestly or illegally not been publicly prosecuted? Greed, arrogance and shady business practices have been ignored for too long. It's time to **iron out** white collar crime.

Business Break 17 March, 2009

Mistaken priorities

When times are tough, the marketing or advertising budget is often the first to go. However, a recent study has shown that consumers are still influenced by marketing and advertising – maybe even more so, as they are being more prudent. If yours is one of the few products they are receiving information about, it is your opportunity to build trust by delivering a quality product to them with excellent service.

So the message is: if you have cut down on your marketing and advertising, you may have **put the cart before the horse**.

Business Bugle 8 February, 2009

NHS groundbreaking report

The long-awaited report on the National Health Service is due at the end of October. This has been the most comprehensive review of the standard of health care in Britain since the 1950s. Let us hope that the government has done its homework: there is a lot of good work going on in our health care system, and the worst-case scenario is that they could **throw the baby out with the bathwater**.

National Echo 6 July, 2008

Top chefs spill the beans

First it was Marco Pierre White who came out of the kitchen closet, confessing that many of his restaurant recipes owed their flavour to the *Knorr* chicken stock cube.
Now other top chefs have admitted their junk food secrets, although these are the snacks they love to eat. For Angela Hartnett, the Michelin-starred head chef at the Connaught, happiness is processed sliced white bread. In the June edition of the BBC's Olive magazine, she says: "Cheap white bread is essential to such British classics as the chip buttie, which I've loved since I was a kid, and the crisp sarnie of course." For Michelin-starred Tom Aikens, life does not get any better than a packet of salt and vinegar crisps. "It's their ultra-acidic and salty flavour combination," he says.

The London Standard 25 May, 2007

Play your cards close to your chest

With a few precautions, the virtual world needn't be any more insecure than the real world. Limit the amount of information available on social networking sites, or simply don't sign up to them at all. When selecting a password for online banking, an email account or any other website for that matter, don't choose something that's obvious or guessable, such as your date of birth…. And whatever you do, NEVER reply to emails from the bank or any other institutions that request confidential information; they would never ask a customer to confirm this information by email.

Weekly Informer 6 February, 2008

Too much of a good thing?

Many employers have stopped websites such as Facebook and MySpace from being accessed at their offices, in the belief that such sites affect a company's productivity. Are they doing the right thing? True, there has been a huge rise in social networking, but maybe that could actually help your business, especially when it comes to searching for new staff. Word of mouth is a proven method of finding employees. Trusting your staff to exercise self restraint in using social websites is less demoralising than imposing an outright ban. Logging on to Facebook is no worse than gossiping in the office; it's just a matter of degree. What is most difficult is knowing when to **draw the line**.

Business Break 3 August, 2009

Don't cut H&S corners in economic downturn

Don't **cut corners** on health and safety during the coming economic downturn – that's the message from Rospa at the start of a week focusing on the prevention of accidents at work.

Roger Bibbings, Rospa occupational safety adviser, said: "Given the current financial climate, there is a danger that occupational health and safety could be seen as a problem largely solved - a 'nice-to-have' rather than a really essential social and economic ingredient. There could be a temptation to **cut corners**, reduce standards or delay introducing essential protective measures."

FM World 21 October, 2008
FM World Magazine and www.fm-world.co.uk are published by Redactive Media Group for the British Institute of Facilities Management

Nailing down your local MP

In theory, your local Parliamentary representative should be contactable face-to-face, by letter or email, or by a phone call. But it is not always so easy. Here are a few tips to increase your chances of discussing any burning issues with your local MP. The ideal scenario is a face-to-face meeting, but remember to give at least one weeks' notice.
Some politicians class emails as on a par with second-class mail. Ensure that your email makes it clear that you live within the constituency. Writing a letter can be more effective. State the topic clearly, keep it clear and brief, use your own words, ask for a response, and avoid (if you can!) being overcritical. Surprisingly, telephoning is generally less successful than writing a letter.

People's Courier 7 October, 2008

Exercises

1 Choose an idiom which can replace the bold words in these sentences.

a) We must make sure we don't **lose the good things** when we replace the old system with the new one. _____

b) I **need to have a frank discussion** with my assistant right now – she sent out the agenda two days late. _____

c) Sorry to interrupt, but I feel it's important to **say what I think** at this point.
_____

d) The quality of the car is really poor. They must have tried to **make it the cheapest way possible**.
_____

e) It will **cause a lot of trouble** when his expenses claims are revealed.
_____

f) I can't deal with this problem myself; I'll have to **get my boss to deal with it**.
_____

2 Complete the mini crossword.

Across

1 There will be a misunderstanding if you get the wrong end of the _ _ _ _ _!

3 Working in the evenings is OK – but I draw the _ _ _ _ at working weekends.

Down

1 You can trust me not to _ _ _ _ _ the beans.

2 We need to _ _ _ _ this out before the next meeting.

3 Which idioms could be used to create sentences which mean the <u>opposite</u> of the sentences below?

a) It's important that we take our time over this project and research it thoroughly.

_____

b) I don't predict any problems in finding new markets.

_____

c) I can trust Ben – he always knows what the priorities are.

_____

d) My manager is always very easy to contact.

_____

e) It's obvious what our competitors are planning to do.

_____

4 **Discussion.**

a) Are you a big fish in a small pond, or a small fish in a big pond? What are the advantages and disadvantages of both?

b) In a negotiation, do you like to play your cards close to your chest?

c) Are you ever tempted to cut corners in your job?

d) Give an example of a time when you had to iron something out.

5 **Combine the words in the box to make five idioms. Use each word only once.**

a	someone's	a	stick	head	fish	wrong	end
nut	the	in	corners	the	a	of	to	bite
crack	small	off	big	hard	pond	cut	

_____

_____

_____

_____

_____

A can of worms

In the 1950s, Canadian/American bait stores sold cans of worms as fishing bait. Fishermen found it easy to open a can of worms, but difficult to close one. This is a modern interpretation of Pandora's Jar, where a mortal was warned not to open Pandora's jar. He opened it and released numerous plagues on the world. So, to open a can of worms means to release a host of (often irrevocable) problems.

Idiom summary

Heads will roll: people will be punished for a mistake made

A fish out of water: feel awkward because you are not familiar with a situation

Stick/poke your nose in: show too much interest in something that does not involve you

A knee-jerk reaction: an instinctive response to something

Stick to your guns: refuse to change or modify your ideas

Two bites of/at the cherry: have a second opportunity to do something

Hot under the collar: angry, resentful or tense

Take the floor: when someone speaks at a conference or meeting

A finger on the pulse: keep up to date with recent developments

Have/get your ducks in a row: have your priorities in the right order

Pie in the sky: something you hope will be achieved, but is unlikely to be

Hear something on the grapevine: discover something by rumour or unofficial source

Money for old rope: an easy way of acquiring money without much effort

Let sleeping dogs lie: warn someone not to talk about a negative situation from the past

Go overboard: too eager, do more than is necessary

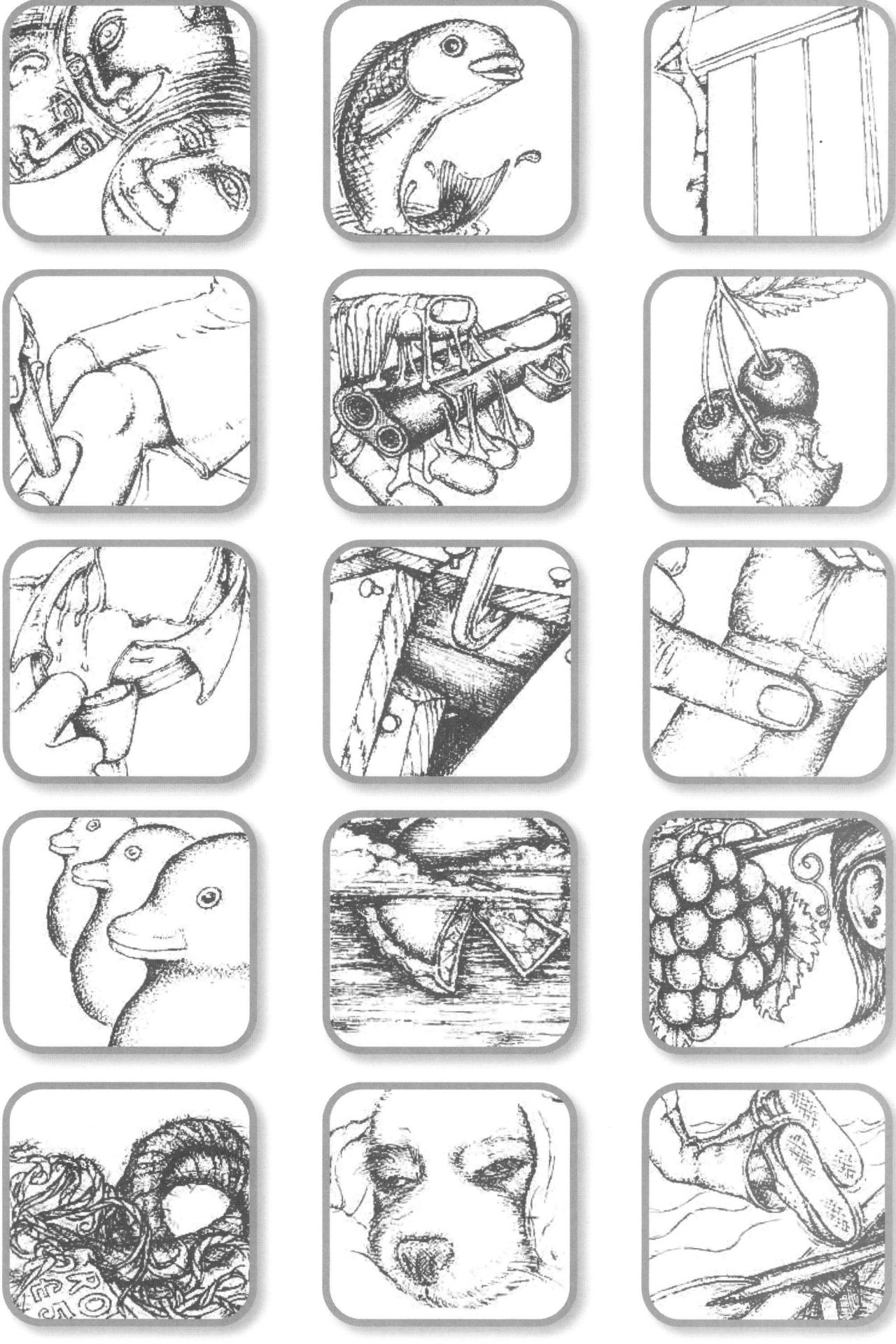

Stick/poke your nose in	A fish out of water	Heads will roll
Two bites of/at the cherry	Stick to your guns	A knee-jerk reaction
A finger on the pulse	Take the floor	Hot under the collar
Hear something on the grapevine	Pie in the sky	Have/get your ducks in a row
Go overboard	Let sleeping dogs lie	Money for old rope

people will be punished for a mistake made

feel awkward because you are not familiar with a situation

show too much interest in something that does not involve you

an instinctive response to something

refuse to change or modify your ideas

have a second opportunity to do something

angry, resentful or tense

when someone speaks at a conference or meeting

keep up to date with recent developments

have your priorities in the right order

something you hope will be achieved, but is unlikely to be

discover something by rumour or unofficial source

an easy way of acquiring money without much effort

warn someone not to talk about a negative situation from the past

too eager, do more than is necessary

Read all about it

Heads will continue to roll

Recent revelations of gross incompetence within several large organisations have led to a record number of CEOs losing their jobs. The *Chief Executive Succession Survey 2005* revealed that the number of Chief Executives dismissed for underperformance has quadrupled in the past ten years. As yet, there is no indication of a decrease in this trend.

Personnel4Now 18 March, 2009

Don't let cold callers leave you hot under the collar

Last year, the government advice service received over 15,000 complaints about cold callers. These included mobile phone contract sales, timeshare, insurance, double glazing and home improvement sellers … Here are a few tips to help you deal with them.

Registering with the Telephone Preference Service should significantly … reduce the number of such calls … If you do speak to a cold caller, don't agree a contract over the phone … If you don't know who you're dealing with, never divulge any financial or personal details … Keep a record of who you are dealing with and how to get hold of them … If you agree to a contract you later regret, you will generally have seven days after you receive written confirmation to cancel.

People's Courier 11 April, 2008

How to resign

New year, new job? When it comes to resigning, remember these few important rules:
- Keep it confidential between you and your boss. Let *him* decide how and when to go public
- Choose the right moment to see your boss
- You don't have to reveal where you're going to be working
- Reassure your boss that you'll be helpful and cooperative if there needs to be a handover period
- Remember your reasons for leaving - **stick to your guns**, even if your decision is not received well.

Daily Recorder 30 January, 2009

Unfair dismissal

The UK's age discrimination legislation came into force in 2006. What protection does the worried senior executive have against his age being a factor in any selection of candidates for redundancy? If he has a disciplinary record, a number of poor appraisals, bad timekeeping, or low productivity, he does not stand much chance, whether he is 31, 41 or 51. But if he is selected for redundancy when a younger colleague is retained, and his performance is at least as good as or better than the younger colleague, there may have been unlawful age discrimination. The key will be how the employer seeks to justify its actions and decisions.

It is therefore essential that employers get their **ducks in a row** when dealing with dismissals so that employees do not think their dismissal is unfair or discriminatory.

Daily Recorder 17 November, 2008

Keep your finger on the pulse

Whether you choose to stay in your current job, or have reason to look for alternative employment, it pays to keep up to date with the events and challenges that are shaping your industry. Hone your networking skills, talk to other professionals within your sector, and also specialist recruitment agencies. This will give you a clearer view of the overall picture, and you can use this as a base for your future decisions.

HR Post 13 December, 2008

The future is here

The more we use renewable energy, the more we benefit the environment, strengthen our energy security, create jobs locally, and help improve our economy. Renewable energy isn't something **pie in the sky**. It's a reality; it's happening right now, and it can create millions of extra jobs and entire new industries if we act soon enough.

Daily Discoverer 7 June, 2008

Tough tactics against equal pay claims

Gender-based pay equality is still a big issue in the workplace, even though the Equal Pay Act came into force nearly 40 years ago. When faced with a claim, employers have two options: 1) to say that the jobs are not comparable, or 2) to demonstrate that the difference in the contract wording is unrelated to gender.

In effect, this gives the employer **two bites of the cherry** and a good chance of defeating any equal pay claim.

Personnel4Now 25 June, 2009

Should I stay or should I go?

Employees today increasingly distrust information received from corporate sources, and question the credibility of those sources. They feel little in terms of company loyalty. And, in many cases, they expect to change jobs several times throughout their careers....

Indeed, employee retention – particularly related to high-performing individuals – is an increasing challenge to corporations around the globe....

Give it to them straight: most companies are more than eager to share good news with their people, and to celebrate success. As our survey confirms, people also want to hear the bad news, no matter how difficult it might be to take. Sooner or later, the word is going to get out. Wouldn't you prefer that your employees **hear it** straight from you than **through the grapevine**? Have a plan to share all of your news with your people. They will trust you more if you are willing to share not only the good, but also the bad and the ugly with them.

www.the-chiefexecutive.com
1 March, 2006
Reprinted with permission from *CEO, Chief Executive Officer*, Global Trade Media (GTM), 2009

Property developers go overboard to shift new homes

Property developers are resorting to increasingly bizarre methods to speed up house sales. The more familiar deals such as discounts for early exchange of contracts, 'free' fitted carpets or white goods, or your mortgage interest paid for a year, are still available. But how does a free professional garden design, a new car in the garage, or a substantial cash-back deal sound? Builders believe that a significant number of people will find such offers irresistible – but are they trying too hard? A realistic selling price must surely be a more acceptable alternative.

Daily Recorder 7 June, 2009

CAD managers must stick their noses in

Have you noticed how CAD managers are often excluded from meetings, planning efforts, new hire orientation, project setups, reviews, and so on? If you are a CAD manager, how do you remedy that? Well, you just have to **stick your nose in**. Doing this sensitively is easier said than done. You may not be good at it at first, but persist and it will get easier. You may even find people start asking you to the meetings – eventually!

Soapbox 2 April, 2009

Coping with culture shock

As well as being a positive, stimulating experience, living in a new culture can also be very challenging. Some people have described it as feeling a bit like being a **fish out of water**.

What kinds of differences will you have to adjust to? As well as a different language, weather and food, you will also have to deal with the different ways people interact with each other, their body language, manners and other cultural behaviours.

'Culture shock' is a natural phenomenon, but after a period of transition it should become easier as you familiarise yourself with the lifestyle of the country.

National Echo 2 May, 2008

Buying new commercial property

Environmental issues are becoming increasingly important for negotiations over business disposals. Many purchasers expect the vendors to enter into a full environmental indemnity. Ideally, you should carry out an audit of the environmental status of the company or business being sold, but on a more realistic level, few vendors are likely to thank you for suggesting that they dig up their factory to discover what, if any, pollutants lie underneath the surface. Sometimes the best advice in these circumstances is to **let sleeping dogs lie**.

Daily Focus 15 May, 2008

Selling your property – beware of the costs

During the housing boom, estate agents typically charge 1 to 1.5% for selling a property - often, from many peoples' point of view, for doing very little. Unfortunately, when estate agents are under pressure, it's customers who suffer with increased charges, which now stand at 2 or 3%.

An estate agent's job is to put together details for a property, put it on the website, produce sales leaflets and photographs, arrange viewings for prospective purchasers and handle negotiations over the price. In practice, sometimes they only have to get the vendor to sign a standard contract, introduce the buyer and charge their commission. In other words, it's **money for old rope**.

Daily Focus 30 April, 2009

Planning a successful conference

Microphones are essential for conference systems where audio recording, transcription or interpretation is required. 'Push To Talk' microphones (PTT) allow delegates at a congress to be heard clearly without interrupting each other.

Each unit contains a high quality digitally controlled microphone and an internal sound system, eliminating the need for external public address systems. They are connected to a central controller which ensures only one delegate can **take the floor** at any one time.

Business Break 22 March, 2009

Hotel trade tactics

What can hotels do to boost trade without investing in costly capital projects, such as installing a gym or a swimming pool? Business travel is the 'bread and butter' of the hotel trade, which is why you can find so many room rate bargains at weekends. But many hotel groups reduce their rates, even for business travellers, as a **knee-jerk reaction** when they want to kick-start their business. It could be argued that all they're doing is giving a cut-price room to people who would probably have gone to their hotel anyway.

Business Break 21 August, 2009

Exercises

1 Which of these phrases are positive and which are negative (from the speaker's point of view)?

a) It's money for old rope! _____

b) He's gone overboard this time. _____

c) It's all pie in the sky, if you ask me. _____

2 Complete the crossword using the clues below.

Across

3   You could feel hot under this when you are asked difficult questions!

4   The type of reaction which is instinctive.

5   Something you stick to when you don't want to change your mind.

Down

1   A row of these means you've got your priorities right.

2   Keep your finger on this if you want to stay ahead.

3   Two bites of which fruit means you get another chance to do something?

3 Who would be most likely to say these remarks (1, 2 or 3)?

a) I think we should let sleeping dogs lie.
   1) Someone who wants to forget about a past problem. ❑
   2) Someone who wants other people to solve a problem for them. ❑
   3) Someone who doesn't want to solve a problem at all. ❑

b) I feel like a fish out of water.
   1) A person who has just been promoted. ❑
   2) A person who thinks he/she is working in the wrong organization. ❑
   3) A person who keeps moving from job to job. ❑

c) Now Tom, I'd like you to take the floor please.
   1) Tom is leaving the meeting. ❑
   2) Tom is going to speak in a meeting. ❑
   3) Tom is going to take the minutes at the meeting. ❑

4 Discussion.

a) Have heads ever rolled in your organisation? Where do you think the expression comes from? Is there a similar expression in your language?

b) How do you feel when someone pokes their nose in? Is it ever justifiable to do this and if so, when? Do you know the expression for a person who does this to expose any improper behaviour?

c) Talk about any occasions when you have needed to keep your finger on the pulse.

d) How reliable is hearing something on the grapevine as a source of accurate information? Can you give any examples?

Hear something on the grapevine

In 1844, when Samuel Morse sent a telegraph message from Washington to Baltimore, the invention was welcomed as a means of broadcasting news rapidly. The term *grapevine telegraph* alluded to the rural poor, whose highly effective verbal communications were compared to the spreading tendrils of the grapevines which they tended.

Idiom summary

Pull the wool over someone's eyes: deceive someone to prevent them knowing the truth

A moveable feast: an event where the time and/or date can be changed

Left high and dry: put in a difficult situation

In at the deep end: facing a problem without enough experience

Put out feelers: make informal enquiries to discover people's opinions

Step out of line: behave inappropriately

Shoot your mouth off: talk too much or indiscreetly

Pour/throw cold water over something: be critical of or negative about something

Swallow a bitter pill: accept an unpleasant or painful necessity

Put your foot in it: accidentally say or do something which causes upset or embarrassment

A cold call: an unexpected call or visit

A sting in the tail: an unpleasant end to something that began well

Lay your cards on the table: be completely honest about your intentions

A storm in a teacup: an overreaction to something unimportant

From the horse's mouth: information obtained from the person directly concerned

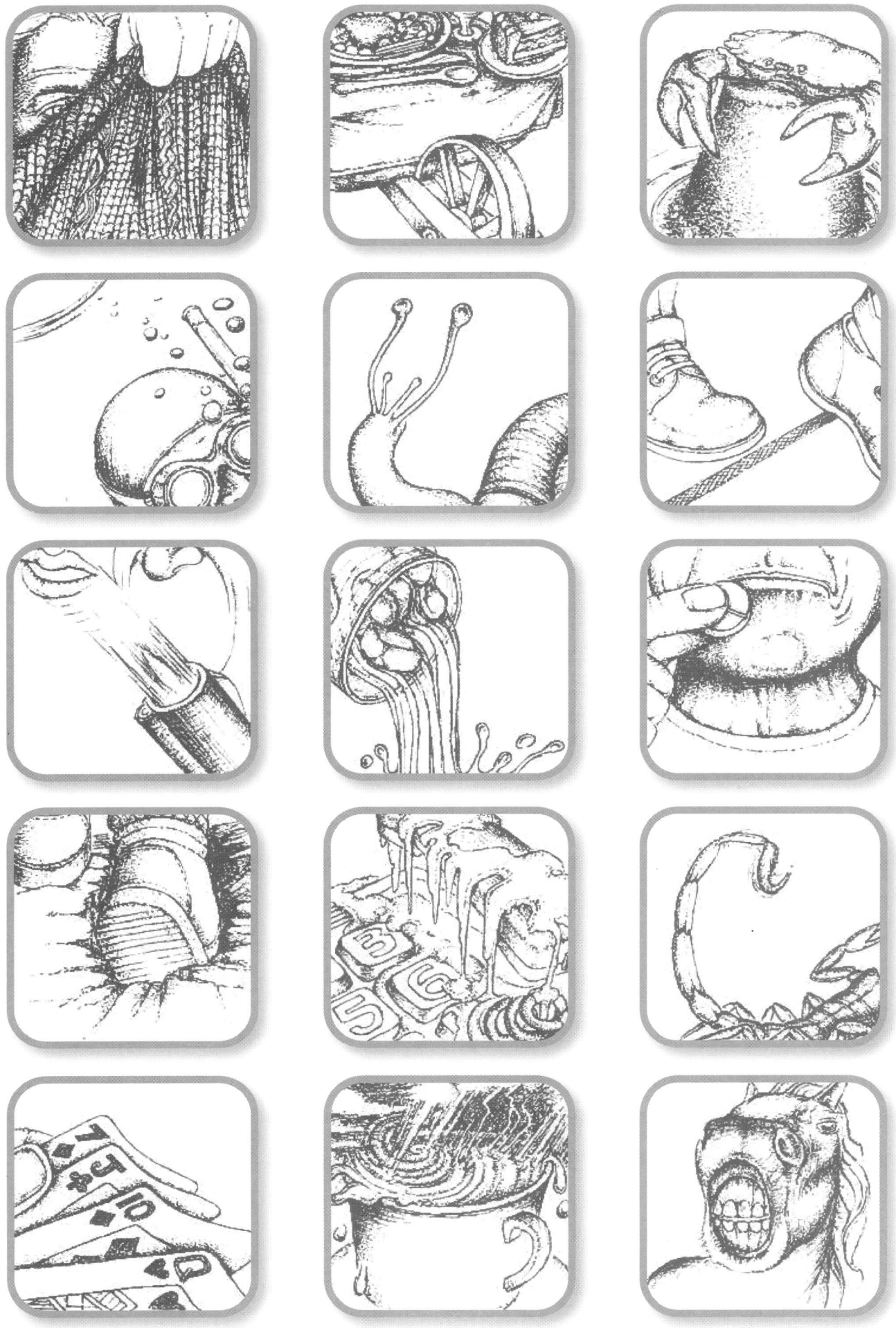

Left high and dry	A moveable feast	Pull the wool over someone's eyes
Step out of line	Put out feelers	In at the deep end
Swallow a bitter pill	Pour/throw cold water on something	Shoot your mouth off
A sting in the tail	A cold call	Put your foot in it
From the horse's mouth	A storm in a teacup	Lay your cards on the table

deceive someone to prevent them knowing the truth

an event where the time and/or date can be changed

put in a difficult situation

facing a problem without enough experience

make informal enquiries to discover people's opinions

behave inappropriately

talk too much or indiscreetly

be critical of or negative about something

accept an unpleasant or painful necessity

accidentally say or do something which causes upset or embarrassment

unexpected call or visit

an unpleasant end to something that began well

be completely honest about your intentions

an overreaction to something unimportant

information obtained from the person directly concerned

Read all about it

Jail for family in wedding con

Members of a Black Country family who married illegal immigrants for money and drugs were today handed jail sentences....

Another two people, including a friend of the family and a Jamaican national who married one of the sons have also been punished for their part in the complex scam....

Judge Robert Orme told the defendants they were part of a sophisticated attempt to **pull the wool over the eyes** of the immigration authorities.

expressandstar.com
19 June, 2009

Tesco rebrands mobile stores as more sites are opened

Tesco has revamped its Telecom stores to 'Phone Shops', in a bid to simplify its stand-alone stores that sell mobile and fixed-line products and services.

There are now 42 specialist stores, and sources claimed Tesco was aiming for between 90 and 100 in 2009. A spokeswoman said it wouldn't be accurate to pinpoint that figure and said that it was '**a moveable feast**'.

Mobile Magazine 26 March, 2008

Insurance exclusions warning

Holidaymakers who buy cheap travel insurance from comparison websites risk being **left high and dry** if they need to make a claim.

Almost half of all travellers buy their travel insurance via an insurance comparison website, but when you read the small print of many policies, you discover that some insurers exclude important elements of cover, including pandemic illness and terrorism.

Daily Focus 18 January, 2009

Making it happen

Nynzi Maung is dedicated to helping women find the confidence to launch a business. Christopher Knox learns why.

Nynzi Maung is pretty down to earth for a high-flying executive who was heavily involved in enhancing international relations between some of the biggest economies in the world.

The multilingual business consultant who runs the Maung Consultancy from her Tyneside home is focused on helping those with the ambition to go it alone.

Originally brought up in Portobello Road in London's Notting Hill, Maung found herself travelling the world as west European executive in the International Division of the London Chamber of Commerce and Industry.

Although she admits that she fell into the job rather than actively pursuing it, her linguistic range, which also included fluent Spanish, ensured that she was a big hit at the chamber. She says: "I was certainly put **in at the deep end** ... I was dealing with a range of companies, ranging from those that made plastic bins to throat lozenges and organising visits around the world to promote the EU's role in fostering international trade."

The Journal 6 July, 2009

Think before you speak

Shooting your mouth off in meetings is a favourite tactic of some managers, who think it demonstrates confidence, competence and leadership qualities. Nothing could be further from the truth, however. At best, you will be regarded as annoying. At worst, people will totally ignore what you are trying to say, even if you are making good suggestions. Know when to shut up. Listen and learn from those who are equally experienced, and respect their views.

Business Break 15 February, 2009

Pincer movement into Russia set to make vodka toast of society

A VODKA made in Scotland is set to become the toast of Russian society when it is served at the Queen's official birthday celebrations at the British Embassy in Moscow later this month.

Pincer vodka will be served to more than 500 Russian dignitaries, including members of parliament and government officials, when the embassy hosts its annual party to celebrate the Queen's birthday on 18 June.

James Barbour, press secretary to the British Embassy said: "It's a big reception and we celebrate it as our national day here, so it will be very interesting to have a Scottish vodka to serve.

... following on from the order from the embassy we have now started to **put out feelers** in Russia and the response has been very positive."

A case of *Pincer*, which is made in Broxburn using Scottish mountain water and elderflower and milk thistle, is now on its way to the embassy in Moscow.

The Scotsman 8 June, 2009

Throwing cold water on government hot air proposals

A business lobby group is worried that government policy does not offer enough subsidies to nuclear power and so-called 'clean coal' technology.... The lobbyists want the government to cut the percentage of energy sourced from wind in targets set for 2020, speed up investment in the electricity grid and get funding in place for Carbon Capture and Storage plants by June 2010.

Daily Focus 1 June, 2009

Swallow the Barnet 'bitter pill' – it will make you better

The idea that a London council like Barnet should be run on the business model of budget airlines is a **hard** [sic] **pill to swallow** for many of the residents in that borough and for most of the country wanting to see what a Cameron government will actually do when in power in under ten months.

Barnet boasts the best schools in the country, some of the most affluent neighbourhoods in London and has produced some of the best business minds in this nation. However Barnet council has also been synonymous with division, not between Labour and Conservative but Conservative against Conservative. Open spats amongst its own councillors over the Icelandic bank fiasco and the freezing of £27.4 million of council money; the open warfare over Barnet Football club; the divisions over wardens in sheltered accommodation, and the list goes on.

The London Daily News, John Kaponi Editor-in-chief

28 August, 2009

Legalities of email disclaimers

Putting a disclaimer at the bottom of an email does not automatically protect you from liability, even though most organisations use email footers as part of their risk mitigation strategy. They are useful as a way of fulfilling a legal obligation to give information or improve an organisation's chance of enforcing its legal rights. However, to be effective, the recipient must be made aware that the exclusion would apply in any business dealings. There is also a problem with enforceability. So don't **put your foot in it**; have any disclaimer checked by a legal specialist before adding it to your correspondence.

Business Bugle

29 November, 2008

Softly, softly reply prolongs misery

How do you respond to **a cold call**? There seem to be as many ways of dealing with them as there are cold calls themselves.

Some people simply slam down the phone immediately.

Others can devote chunks of the day to politely spurning such calls ("after all, they have a job to do").

Probably the most common reaction amongst British people is the guilt-trip response; you listen to what the caller has to say, then spend precious time politely explaining that you already have/do not want/do not need the product or service they are offering.

People's Courier 17 August, 2009

Housing fund has 'sting in the tail'

Northumberland County Council's economic prosperity committee heard that under the government's new 'Kickstart Housing Development Fund', 225 units could be built in Blyth, Ashington and Alnwick.

The aim of the fund, councillors heard, is to restart housing schemes that have stalled because of the economic recession and provide more new affordable housing.

However, this change in emphasis means 550 homes in the private sector waiting for council-funded improvements may not receive them.

Housing services manager for the private sector Martin Laidler… said that the changes in government priority affecting the 550 homes on the waiting list, homes he described as 'vulnerable', was a **'sting in the tail'**.

The News Post Leader

10 August, 2009

Millom's future – cards on the table

THE group charged with regenerating Millom will publicly **lay its** financial **cards on the table** for the first time.

Millom and Haverigg Economic Development Group will display the 'exit report' for the Market Town Initiative at next month's Millom Town Council meeting.

The report details when and where money was spent during the three year MTI project, which included refurbishment plans for Millom Palladium.

The move follows a renewed effort by the group to promote transparency and openness with the public over its plans.

The report is being shown at the meeting on November 26 at the request of Millom Town Council.

North-West Evening Mail

22 October, 2008

Burt apportions blame

Sir Peter Burt, the former deputy chairman of HBOS, has rejected criticism of his role in the bank's demise. Following the revelation of nearly eleven billion pound losses at HBOS, Burt dismissed speculation about Lloyds Banking Group being nationalised, as '**a storm in a teacup**'.

He admitted that HBOS was in a mess, but said he was puzzled as to why nationalisation was being mooted. "On the basis of the figures we have seen to date, there is plenty of capital, and the underlying ratios are quite strong."

Daily Focus 1 February, 2009

Google drops 80/20 search bomb

At the Great B2B Marketing Debate, where SEO (search engine optimisation) went head to head against PPC (pay per click) and won, Stuart Small from Google let drop a bomb of immense proportions – Google knows that 80 per cent of searchers click on a natural result and 20 per cent click on a paid listing. …

Suddenly SEMs have a number, provided by Google, about how important having a natural listing is. This is no longer an area of speculation – we have the number **from the horse's mouth**.

Technology Weekly

18 December, 2007

Has your blogging got you into trouble at work?

An estimated 30% of UK bloggers are at risk of getting the sack because of derogatory comments they've written about their boss or colleagues.

So, if you MUST blog about your company and/or your superiors, don't use your real name on the blog. Conversely, make sure your boss reads your blog, so that he or she can give me you an early warning if they think you have **stepped out of line**.

Daily Focus 9 May, 2008

Exercises

Richard is in his local employment office telling the story of what happened to him recently, and speaking quite formally. Rewrite the story as an email to a friend, using idioms to replace the phrases in bold, to make it less formal.

When I started my last job they didn't tell me I would have to **sell to people who had not even asked to speak to me**. I was **in a difficult position** because I needed the money, so I **accepted the situation** and got to work.

But to be honest, I found it difficult to **deceive people** by trying to sell them something unsuitable. I would **be completely open and truthful with them** so that they could make an informed choice. Eventually, my boss heard about this and asked me to report to his office. I knew then that, in his opinion, I had **been making a big mistake**.

He said I was not working in line with company policy, so I told him that I thought his business procedures were dishonest; that I believed it was best to **discover what people really needed**, rather than try to pressurize them into buying something.

Unfortunately, he **rejected** my opinions and started **telling me just what he thought of me**! He ended by saying that if I continued to **do things my way,** I would find myself **in a very difficult situation**. I knew exactly what he meant.

Hearing all this coming **directly from the boss** made me realize that I didn't want the job at all, so I resigned immediately. But there was a **final unpleasant event**. The day I was due to receive my salary, it wasn't paid into my bank account. When I phoned the company to find out what had happened, they said my payment would be a couple of days late. This happened three times before I finally got paid. I was not surprised to discover that payday was **a flexible event** because the company was having cashflow problems. In the end, everything turned out to be **an unnecessary worry**. I knew then that the new job I've got is much better, and at a higher salary too!'

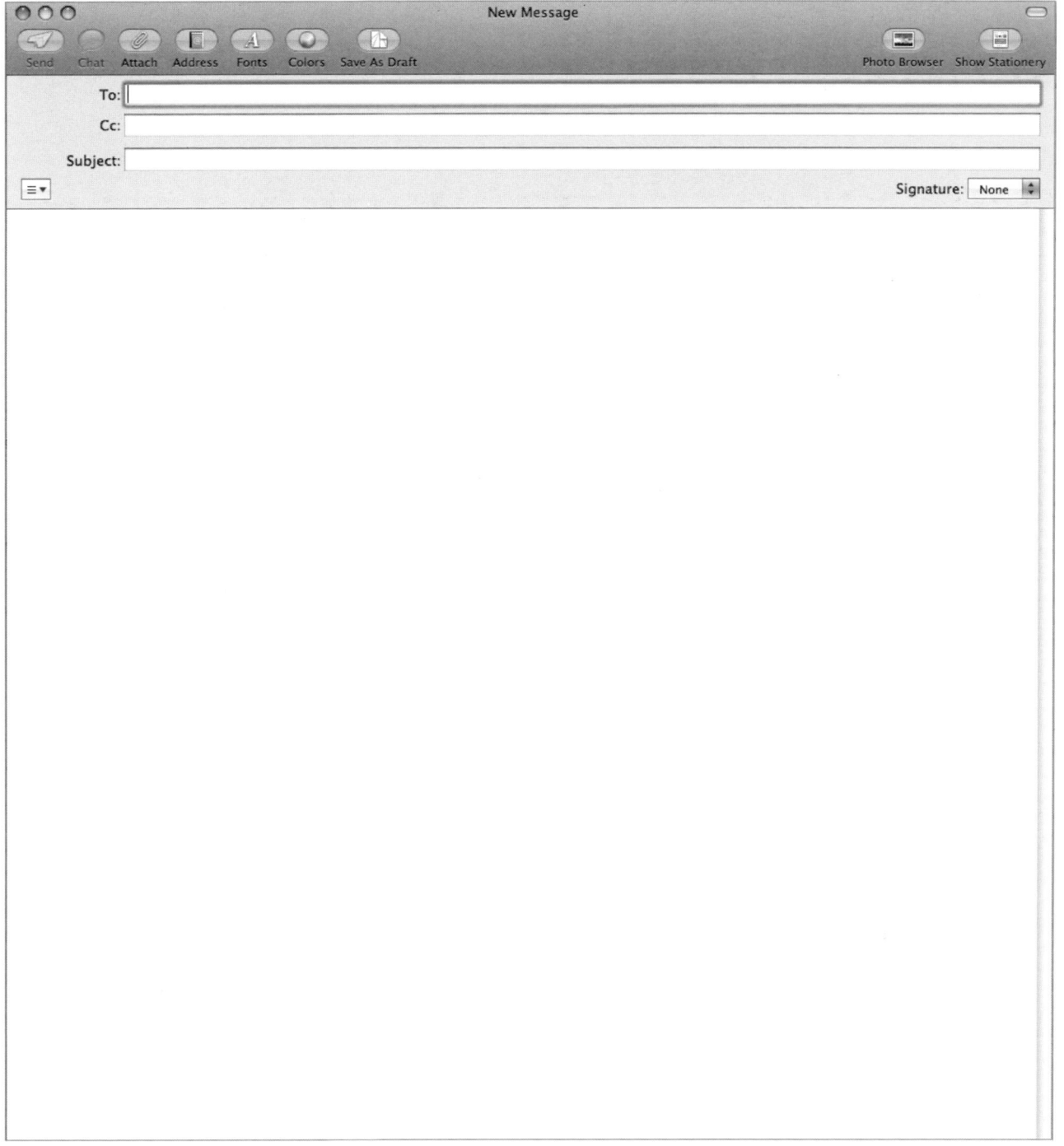

Pull the wool over someone's eyes

Wool was slang for *hair*, synonymous with the powdered wigs worn by gentlemen several centuries ago. The most powerful men with the most elaborate hairstyles became our first *bigwigs*. When a *bigwig* took a stroll down a city street, young criminals would pull the wig (wool) down over the gentleman's eyes, so they could steal his wallet.

Idiom summary

Blow the whistle: report something negative so that it can be stopped

It's in the bag: something that will definitely be achieved

The last straw: a final, extra difficulty, which makes a situation impossible

Run it up the flagpole: tell people about an idea to get their opinion

Paint yourself into a corner: do something which puts you in an awkward situation

Rise to the bait: react to something in the way that another person wanted

In hot water: in trouble or in a difficult situation

The ball is in someone's court: making someone else the first to take responsibility

Grasp the nettle: take immediate action to deal with something difficult

In the driving seat: in control of something

In a nutshell: summarizing a situation

Have egg on your face: be embarrassed because of something stupid you have done

In the loop: be kept fully informed about developments

The balloon's gone up: something becomes very serious or unpleasant

A foot in the door: do a small thing to create an opportunity in the future

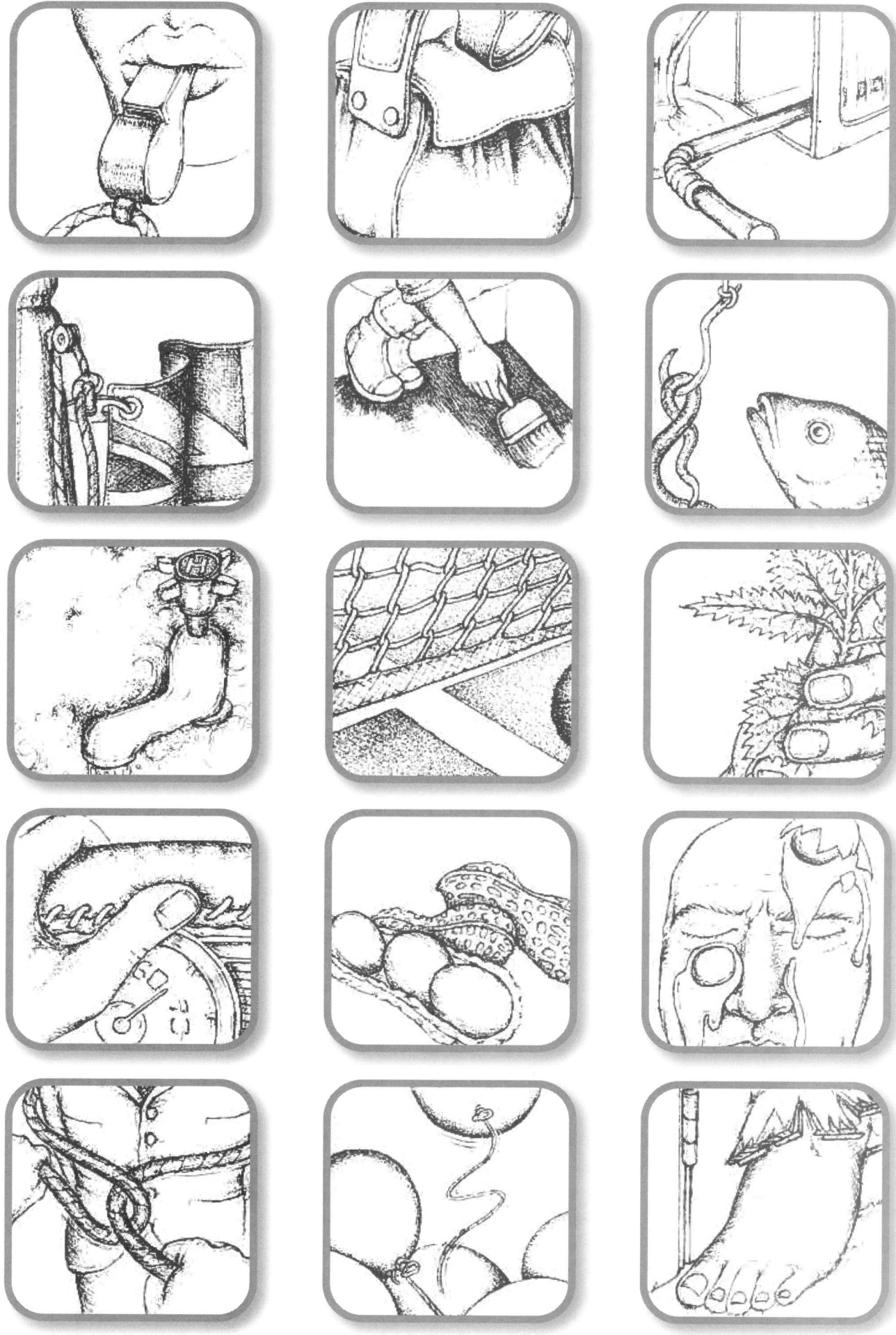

The last straw	It's in the bag	Blow the whistle
Rise to the bait	Paint yourself into a corner	Run it up the flagpole
Grasp the nettle	The ball is in someone's court	In hot water
Have egg on your face	In a nutshell	In the driving seat
A foot in the door	The balloon's gone up	In the loop

report something negative so that it can be stopped	something that will definitely be achieved	a final, extra difficulty, which makes a situation impossible
tell people about an idea to get their opinion	do something which puts you in an awkward situation	react to something in the way that another person wanted
in trouble or in a difficult situation	making someone else the first to take responsibility	take immediate action to deal with something difficult
in control of something	summarizing a situation	be embarrassed because of something stupid you have done
be kept fully informed about developments	something becomes very serious or unpleasant	do a small thing to create an opportunity in the future

Read all about it

Are nurses who fail to blow the whistle on bad practice protecting themselves?

YES (Nigel Jopson)

It is never easy to **blow the whistle** but, at times, it is the only way to move things forward. We surely did not come into nursing to tolerate seeing people abused or damaged, deliberately or by neglect.

We need to be fully prepared to stand up for our patients. It is easier to stop an individual who is causing harm intentionally or by a lack of training than it is to change the way an institution behaves.

NO (Ian Pierce-Hayes)

As nurses, our first consideration must be the interests and safety of patients. However, the whole notion of whistle-blowing is often far from clear-cut and the recriminations for those who have been brave enough to raise their concerns can be so severe and bitter that it can lead to an atmosphere of fear and intimidation that prevents any discussion – let alone criticism – of practice.

Nursing Times 28 May, 2008

Surviving under stress

Fed up with being harassed by your boss? Do you ever feel like telling him what you really think? Before you say something you may later regret, here are three golden rules for controlling your temper:

First, don't **rise to the bait** - take a deep breath and count to ten.

Second, remember that you have to face this person tomorrow. And the day after that, and the day after that…

Finally, ask yourself: is it *really* worth getting so upset over a job?

Personnel4Now 7 September, 2009

ID cards – for or against?

No wonder there is so much resistance to ID cards in the UK. Ideas currently being **run up the flagpole** could result in a total surveillance system. Future generations of cashpoints and point of sale equipment could incorporate biometrics and ID cards. ID checks in association with financial transactions to combat identity fraud would mean people having to use their ID card several times a day. Add to this the ID checks of the National Identity Register, and the Government would have not only revenue, but also detailed records of everybody's financial transactions and whereabouts.

Northern Reporter 14 July, 2009

Keep cleaners in the loop to fight spread of swine flu

… Pete Clutterbuck, operations director of waste management and cleaning company Waste Efficiency Ltd of Hallow, said: … "NHS and HPA guidelines say if anyone is unwell with flu-like symptoms, they should self-isolate at home to reduce the risk of the virus spreading to other people. However, cleaners usually cannot possibly know who is ill in an office, school or factory. They do their job late in the evening after everyone has gone home, so do not know what's happened in the preceding hours. Our request to employers is to try to keep the cleaners informed by putting a simple desk or work area sign up if anyone has had to self-isolate. This can alert the cleaners to ensure that all nearby hard surfaces are cleaned thoroughly as a priority."

He said: "Professional and thorough cleaning regimes are very much a weapon in the fight against the spread of the disease, and by taking just a few seconds to keep the cleaner **in the loop**, we hope it can make a difference."

Worcester News 27 July, 2008
Abridged article reproduced courtesy of the *Worcester News*

Government prop for small businesses

In recent months, well-known companies with financial difficulties have collapsed after the removal of credit insurance proved to be **the last straw**. The government is planning to introduce a multibillion-pound scheme to help the many companies that are struggling to secure crucial business insurance.

Economics Daily 2 January, 2009

How to resign

After looking for a new job while you're still employed, accepting an offer comes as a huge relief. At last, you're free! But remember – your departure must be as strategic as your arrival.

Never disclose that you're leaving before you have a signed agreement and official start date from your new employer. Always tell your immediate superior first. If you blab to everyone and your job offer falls through, you will have **egg on your face**.

Business Break 2 November, 2008

Office emails can land you in hot water

HAVE you ever made an inappropriate comment about a colleague in an email and forwarded it to that person by accident? Or written a confidential e-mail but then accidentally hit 'reply to all' when you only meant to hit 'reply'?

Sending an email in error can be a minor embarrassment - or it can cost you your job.

Yet, with some two million emails sent globally every second, it's no wonder that most of us have, at some time, forgotten our netiquette and committed an email faux pas which has ended up causing offence, embarrassment, annoyance or even got us the sack.

Shropshire Star 17 April, 2008

Learning the tricks of the trade

… Award-winning reporter, broadcaster and trainer Andrew Glover has built a respected reputation for his work with the BBC, Trinity Mirror Group and Border Television, and he is now offering multimedia services with his own company *Lush Places Media*.

The Teesdale-based company hosts workshops for companies who want to improve digital awareness and make the most of videos, social networking and podcasting, as well as dealing with the media 'when the balloon goes up'.

Southern Reporter
18 June, 2009

Patent ball in Microsoft's court

A US judge has ordered Microsoft Corp. to stop selling copies of its flagship word-processing software, Word, because it wilfully infringed on a patent held by a small Canadian company.

Microsoft said it plans to appeal, but the i4i chairman Loudon Owen says his company remains willing to work out a deal with the software giant. "**The ball is in their court**. If Microsoft wants to get hold of us, they have our phone number."

Business Break 20 August, 2009

Job interview: money issues

Traditionally, the British are reluctant to raise the subject of money in an interview. It is usually not discussed until the latter stages of recruitment. Indeed, many employers are put off by would-be employees asking about salary at too early a stage.

Always be truthful about your current salary. You may also be asked how much you want to be paid. If you go in with too high a figure, the danger is that you will frighten off the prospective employer. Too low, and you will **paint yourself into a corner**. Do your research, be realistic in your expectations, and you'll have the job **in the bag**.

Monthly Jobsround
26 February, 2008

Time to grasp the nettle over safety

HEADTEACHER Helen Johnson and her governors are concerned about the safety of pupils on the busy road outside their school. Colton Primary in Leeds is on a narrow lane so it is understandable that currently there are worries about a bus which has been routed past the building….

Mrs Johnson's fear is that sooner or later a child will be killed or seriously injured on the road near the school, which has 250 pupils but does not qualify for a formal crossing point….

The bus company's argument is that traffic management in general needs to be improved, and that if buses are struggling to get down the road then the same could apply to emergency vehicles.

All of which highlights that there is a bigger picture and a bigger issue to be considered here: that parents themselves now cause problems outside almost all schools by parking there while they drop off children. It is an ongoing problem that shows no real sign of being improved.

Perhaps the time has come to **grasp the nettle** and look at real solutions, which could even mean banning parking outside schools, rather than tinkering at the edges of a situation that poses a threat to our sons and daughters.

Yorkshire Evening Post
9 July, 2009
Reproduced by kind permission of the *Yorkshire Evening Post*.

Government in the driving seat of electric car revolution

The Prime Minister recently announced that trials for electric cars are expected to begin next year in cities across the UK. Councils will be invited to submit bids to become one of Britain's first 'green cities'. Ministers will also meet electricity suppliers to discuss developing a national network of roadside power points where vehicles can recharge their batteries.

Northern Reporter
19 April, 2009

Innovation in a nutshell

Innovation is critical to the survival of any business. And while there are now a thousand definitions of the phrase, this one – from Deka Research president Dean Kamen – is telling: "It's like getting a Sumo wrestler to look good in a tutu."

… The 10 stages of innovation:
1. Scepticism
2. Enthusiasm
3. Brass band and fireworks
4. Results aren't visible
5. Existing business suffering
6. Is it worth it?
7. Start to see pay offs
8. This is taking time
9. Maybe not a bad idea
10. It works!

Eureka Magazine
15 January, 2007

Funds now in London to finance Sheffield Wednesday takeover

THE man behind a proposed bid to buy control of Sheffield Wednesday acknowledges he did provide proof of funding from an offshore bank in Dominica – but insists the money behind the takeover was always based in a Swiss bank account.

Geoff Sheard, who denied the Dominica connection in Saturday's Yorkshire Post, said he produced a letter from the Private Capital Bank as a means of getting a '**foot-in-the-door**' to open talks. He said a friend owns the bank.

Dismissing the Dominica link as 'irrelevant', Sheard said: "I think a lot of things have happened since that document came out – that was a get a foot-through-the-door document but it has nothing to do with the purchase of the football club and nothing to do with the source of funding. The money is from a Swiss bank."

Yorkshire Post 26 August, 2008
Reproduced by kind permission of the *Yorkshire Post*.

Exercises

1 Tick (✓) the box if the idioms are correct. If the idioms are incorrect, rewrite them.

a) Before we put the idea into practice, we should paint the flagpole. ❏

_____

b) I've put off applying for a promotion for too long. It's time to cut the nettle. ❏

_____

c) I had egg on my face when I handed out the wrong figures at the sales meeting. ❏

_____

2 Match the newspaper headlines with the texts (there are more texts than headlines).

1) **Blow the whistle on cheats** ❏   2) **Government in hot water** ❏

3) **Last straw for small enterprises** ❏   4) **Pupils in the driving seat** ❏

A The organization which oversees anti-doping programmes in sport yesterday urged anyone with links to those suspected of using illegal performance-enhancing drugs to name the guilty parties.

B The telecoms company has offered a generous early redundancy package to 100 employees. It's now up to them to decide whether they will accept it or not.

C This newspaper has discovered another national scandal. 'There will be a number of people in a lot of trouble over this' said a spokesperson.

D Raising taxes again is going to be the final difficulty in a series of problems for these people; and something from which some of them will never recover.

E Yesterday, youngsters from the Medway Primary swapped roles with their teachers for a day, to raise money for charity.

F Unions yesterday announced they were confident that their pay claim was going to be accepted without opposition.

3 Two of the texts from Exercise 2 did <u>not</u> have a headline. Can you think of a suitable headline for these texts? Use idioms from this section of the book, or any other idioms you know.

_____

_____

4 Discussion.

a) Getting your first job can be difficult. What advice would you give to college leavers to help them get a foot in the door?

b) What are the problems associated with keeping too many people in the loop?

c) Have you ever painted yourself into a corner? What was the outcome?

d) Is it right to blow the whistle on your employer? If your answer is yes, in what circumstances would *you* be a whistleblower?

e) Name some of the circumstances which could get an employee into hot water.

5 Match each statement on the left with the most likely response on the right.

a) I'm pretty sure we've won the contract. ❏

b) My boss insists that men are brighter than women. ❏

c) This is our best and final offer. ❏

d) Jack's work is poorly presented, always late and incomplete. ❏

e) Have you heard the latest government scandal? ❏

f) What do you think of the new incentive scheme? ❏

1) Yes, the ball's in the union's court now.

2) In a nutshell, he needs to make a lot more effort.

3) Let's run it up the flagpole before we put it into practice.

4) Yes, I think it's in the bag.

5) I have – when the press got hold of the story the balloon went up.

6) My advice is: don't rise to the bait

Blow the whistle

The term *whistleblower* derives from the practice of English 'bobbies' (police), who would blow their whistles when they were alerted to a crime. The whistle would summon their fellow officers and warn the general public of any danger.

Idiom summary

Nip it in the bud: stop a problem at an early stage

A hatchet job: making strong and unfair criticism of something

Drive someone up the wall: make someone very angry or irritated

A glass ceiling: unacknowledged limitation on promotion at work

Eat humble pie: admit you are wrong and apologize

Lose the thread: be unable to follow what is being said or done

Turn up the heat: intensify pressure on a person or situation

At the sharp end: the most challenging part of an activity

Doesn't hold water: something that can be proved to be wrong

Scrape the barrel: use something of poor quality because there is no choice

Bite your tongue: stop yourself saying something inappropriate

Strike while the iron is hot: act quickly on a good opportunity

A thorn in someone's side: a source of continuous annoyance or trouble

Keep your feet on the ground: retain your personality, despite fame or success

Off the record: saying something you do not want to be publicly known

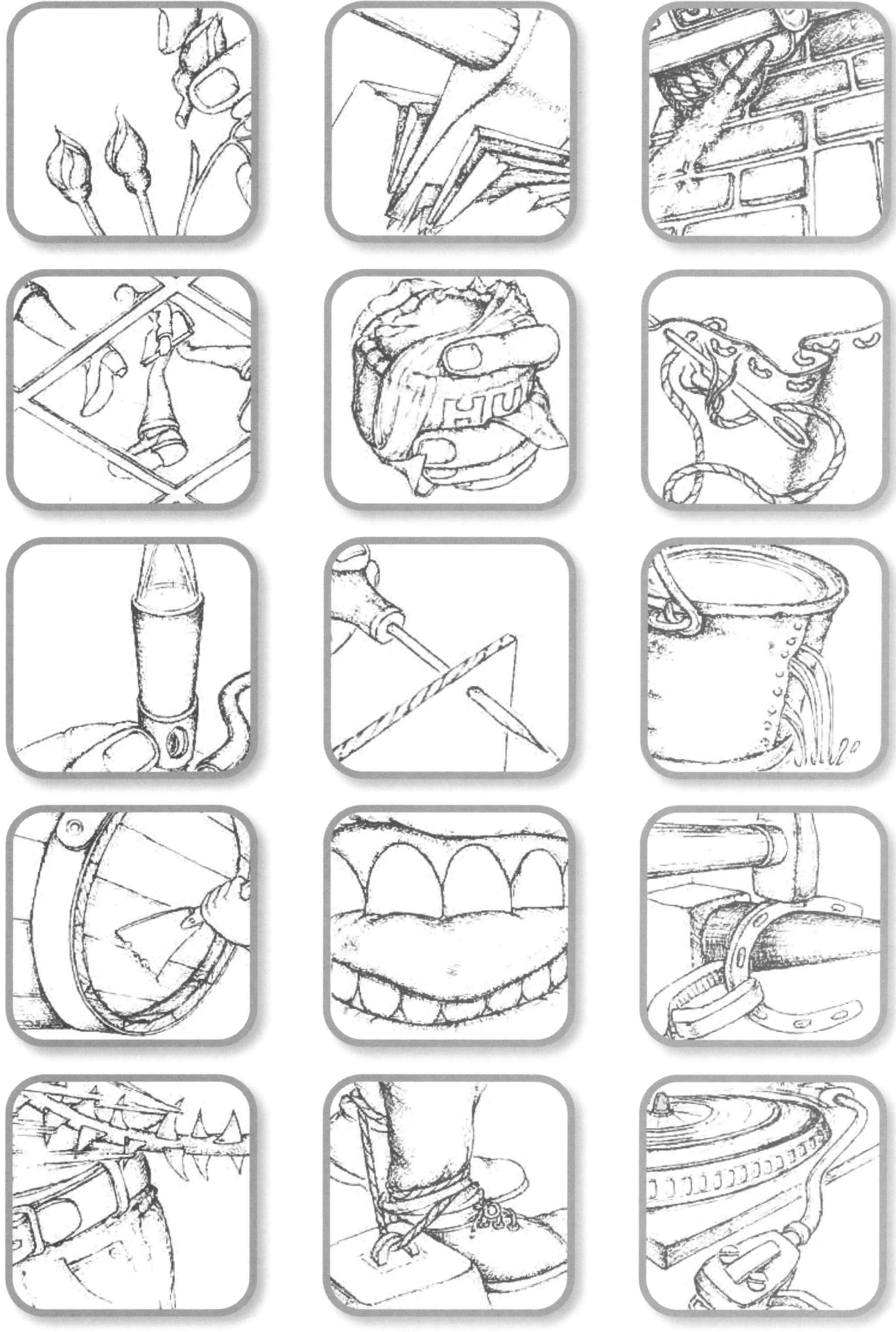

Drive someone up the wall	**A hatchet job**	**Nip it in the bud**
Lose the thread	**Eat humble pie**	**A glass ceiling**
Doesn't hold water	**At the sharp end**	**Turn up the heat**
Strike while the iron is hot	**Bite your tongue**	**Scrape the barrel**
Off the record	**Keep your feet on the ground**	**A thorn in someone's side**

stop a problem at an early stage	making strong and unfair criticism of something	make someone very angry or irritated
unacknowledged limitation on promotion at work	admit you are wrong and apologize	be unable to follow what is being said or done
intensify pressure on a person or situation	the most challenging part of an activity	something that can be proved to be wrong
use something of poor quality because there is no choice	stop yourself saying something inappropriate	act quickly on a good opportunity
a source of continuous annoyance or trouble	retain your personality, despite fame or success	saying something you do not want to be publicly known

Read all about it

Act fast to prevent official grievances

An unhappy shop-floor worker means unhappy customers, so retailers must **nip** grievances **in the bud**. Retailers rely on their front-line staff to be the face of their brand. If your staff have a grievance, it can very quickly become clear to the customer and have an impact on service and sales. Managers should be trained to look out for the signs of an unhappy employee.

Business Break 8 January, 2008

Mobile phone charges under scrutiny

Text messaging overpriced? Are mobile phone charges ripping off the customer? If you think so, tune into the BBC's Dispatches programme next week, which will be **a hatchet job** on the UK mobile industry.

Soapbox 6 May, 2009

The recession – strike while the iron is hot

The time for small businesses to expand is right now, not next month or next year. Take advantage of the price cuts... we already know prices are going to increase.

Begin your research online for business financing options. If you have strong business credit it is a plus, but alternative financing is not limited to the banks that just look at credit. Peer-to-Peer lending sites, merchant circles, and other social media outlets offer plenty of opportunity to find a way to get the money you need to expand.

Business Break 26 May, 2009

Scrap school league tables

A new report by the Institute for Public Policy Research warns that school league tables of pupils' exam scores should be scrapped as they have become a poisonous **thorn in the side** of educational progress.

Announcing the new primary strategy in May this year, Charles Clarke, the Secretary of State for Education, said that "testing, targets and performance tables are very much here to stay".

Daily Discoverer 2 May, 2009

Eating humble pie

Have you ever made a mistake in business? Perhaps something silly that has a consequence for your client? How do you admit the error to your client and still come out looking good in their eyes? First of all, act promptly: the sooner you take action, the better your clients will receive the news. Be honest: honesty breeds respect. It is also a good idea to have a plan to rectify the mistake before you speak to your clients. This is a great time to offer a service or product to your client – it is a sign of acknowledging the inconvenience caused to them. And finally, be gracious: your client may be upset about the mistake. Accept their reactions graciously – they will pass if you show genuine remorse.

Business Break 2 January, 2009

Difficulties in the office

What **drives you up the wall** at work? The most common complaints are about someone who:
- always talks about personal issues
- always misses deadlines
- goes off sick regularly, making more work for their colleagues
- complains and is negative about the company all the time
- is always late for meetings
- eats hot, smelly food (such as burgers and chips) in the office

It is estimated that at least 15 per cent of workers say their co-workers' constant complaining drives them crazy, and the same number say colleagues passing off their work is frustrating.

Economics Daily 2 January, 2009

Rise in e-crime

E-criminals are **turning up the heat** on businesses fighting digital crime: more than 3.5 million online crimes were committed in the UK last year. The black market for credit cards, passports, personal details and so on has doubled, and digital crimes are becoming increasingly sophisticated.

Sixty-eight per cent of companies said they are forced to spend up to 40% of their security budget protecting themselves against high-tech criminals.

Business Break 4 February, 2009

How to have without prejudice off-the-record discussions safely

With the global recession, credit crunch and potential property crash on the horizon, employers will no doubt be looking to restructure and reorganise their organisations with resultant dismissals.

Often, and particularly at senior level, employers do not wish to go through a lengthy, time-consuming procedure and instead will use 'without prejudice' or '**off the record**' approaches to negotiate an employee's departure. However, difficulties arise when an employee refuses to do a deal and instead attempts to rely on the details of the negotiations as the basis of a claim. …

As long as it is properly handled, however, it should still be possible for employers to approach employees on a without prejudice basis rather than go through what could be a damaging, time-consuming and pointless disciplinary or dismissal procedure.

Employers' Law
15 September, 2008

Promotion in perspective

A promotion isn't a reason to change your personality. Don't lose sight of where you came from, or those who helped you reach this next stage. Make an effort to maintain existing friendships and contacts, as this will help to **keep your feet on the ground**.

Business Break 3 December, 2008

Onwards and upwards

You applied for a new job. You survived the arduous interview process, the psychometric tests and all the other challenges they set you. But it's key to remind your future boss just how vital your contribution will be to the future of his company when it gets to **the sharp end** of proceedings. Accept a salary offer and things won't look up much from there unless you get promoted. Changing jobs can be a very good opportunity to improve your lot financially.

Business Break 16 January, 2009

An inevitable crisis

Europe's sub-prime crisis has now hit home as heavily-indebted nations of the eastern bloc are turning to the IMF. The theory that these nations now have a thriving economy independent of the rest of the world just **doesn't hold water**. These countries have been dependent on consumer spending in America and Europe all along - and now that western consumers are staying away from the shops, no one is buying their goods. What is needed is an international central bank which can provide liquidity guarantees, recapitalise banks and regulate international financial flows.

National Courier 28 March, 2008

Too much of a good thing

Is it acceptable to use laptops in meetings? I think it's fair to say that laptops cause meetings to be longer and less productive (unless they have to be used to access diagrams, etc.).

Apparently, if you are distracted for only 10 seconds you can **lose the thread** and aren't properly involved any more. Even checking your email often takes more than ten seconds, as does almost any other laptop task.

Business Bugle 20 October, 2008

Ministers' desperate measures

After the recent revelations by government ministers regarding misuse of taxpayers' money, the ministers are starting to **scrape the bottom of the barrel**, using selected information taken out of context to suit their headlines.

The scandal started after the revelation that ministers had been making false or exaggerated claims for housing expenses. MPs expenses are due to be published on parliament's website later this month. People will then be able to see for themselves how their money has been spent.

Daily Focus 28 June, 2009

Women architects 'still face glass ceiling'

Nearly three-quarters of all women architects believe their careers could be checked by **a glass ceiling**, according to a new survey.

The study, carried out for consultant Atkins, also shows that almost half of female architects have experienced gender inequalities in the workplace.

The poll, which quizzed 3,300 men and women across a range of disciplines, including architecture, found that 19.5 per cent of female architects claim **a glass ceiling** 'definitely exists' and 53 per cent believe it is 'potentially there'. It also found that 11 per cent of women architects 'frequently' experience inequalities, while a further 34 per cent experience them 'occasionally'.

The Architects' Journal
15 July, 2007

Don't talk yourself out of a job

Even though executive-level candidates are unquestionably more polished and sophisticated today than they used to be, it is surprising how many basic interview etiquette mistakes are still made.

Common mistakes included a lack of knowledge about the company or position, over-inflated ego and appearing overconfident.

However, talking too much is cited as the most common interview mistake made by job seekers, even those applying for executive level positions. This can often be due to eagerness to get the job, or simply nervousness. The key is to listen to yourself; if you think you are 'rambling' on about irrelevant information, **bite your tongue**. The interviewer will ask you anything else he needs to know.

Business Break 1 February, 2009

Exercises

1 **What idioms could you use in the following situations?**

a) You are in a meeting with native English speakers and everyone starts interrupting each other, which makes it very difficult for you.

_____

b) You are a woman who is very good at your job. You keep trying for a promotion, but for some reason you are always unsuccessful.

_____

c) You shout at one of your employees because he has not handed in his weekly report on time. Later, you discover you have filed it away by mistake.

_____

d) You have offered a customer a very good deal, and now need to do something to encourage them to make up their mind.

_____

e) A work colleague is always 'borrowing' your pens and never returns them.

_____

2 **Discussion.**

a) If you are scraping the barrel, are you:
   i)   conscientious and thorough?   ❏
   ii) desperate?   ❏
   iii) dealing with unimportant issues? ❏

b) Do you ever lose the thread when you are in a foreign business meeting? What types of words should you listen for when you are trying to follow a conversation? What is the general name given to such words?

c) Give some examples of what drives you up the wall. Do _you_ ever drive people up the wall?

d) In which situation(s) is it better to bite your tongue? Do you have similar sayings in your own language?

3 The wordsearch below contains key words from seven idioms from this section. The definitions of the idioms are listed below to help you. The words can appear horizontally, vertically, diagonally, from left to right or right to left.

a) stop a problem at an early stage
b) use something of poor quality because there is no choice
c) strong and unfair criticism of something
d) retain your personality despite fame or success
e) the most challenging part of an activity
f) something that can be proved to be wrong
g) react quickly to a good opportunity

P	B	F	P	R	A	H	S
W	A	T	E	R	O	A	C
E	R	N	I	E	S	T	R
N	R	I	R	E	T	C	A
D	E	C	O	O	O	H	P
T	L	B	N	U	H	E	E
G	R	O	U	N	D	T	K
A	L	J	H	D	N	I	P

4 Complete the idiom with the correct words from the box.

a) **A:** I'm so angry, I feel like telling our manager just what I think of him!
B: I think it would be wise to bite your _____ until the next departmental meeting.

b) **A:** We're under huge pressure to create a working prototype in a short time.
B: I suggest we put Kate in charge of the project – she always loves being at the _____ end.

c) **A:** Have the clients responded to our proposal yet?
B: No, I think it's time to turn up the _____ and tell them another company is interested.

d) They say Bob's not in work because he's sick. But just off the _____, I've heard he's been suspended because made a false claim for hotel expenses.

e) **A:** The union is encouraging the staff to go on strike.
B: Let's have a meeting to discuss their complaints, then hopefully we can nip it in the _____.

Nip it in the bud

This term originates from horticulture, when it was discovered that better fruit is produced if surplus buds are removed from a tree or bush. When the bud is removed, it will obviously be prevented from developing.

Idiom summary

Go down like a lead balloon: a comment or suggestion which is not received well

Push the envelope: extend the limits of performance

Tie yourself in knots: become very confused when you try to explain something

The thin end of the wedge: the start of a bigger, more harmful development

Wide of the mark: be wrong about something

A cock and bull story: a story or explanation which is obviously untrue

Between a rock and a hard place: having to make a choice between two unpleasant options

Pick someone's brains: ask for advice from someone more knowledgeable

Sing from the same song sheet: present a united front

Water off a duck's back: criticism which has no effect on somebody

Add fuel to the fire: make an argument or bad situation worse

The gloves are off: something will be resolved in an unpleasant way

A shot in the arm: give encouragement/boost morale

Move the goalposts: change the rules unfairly

Fly by the seat of your pants: make decisions as you go along, without a plan

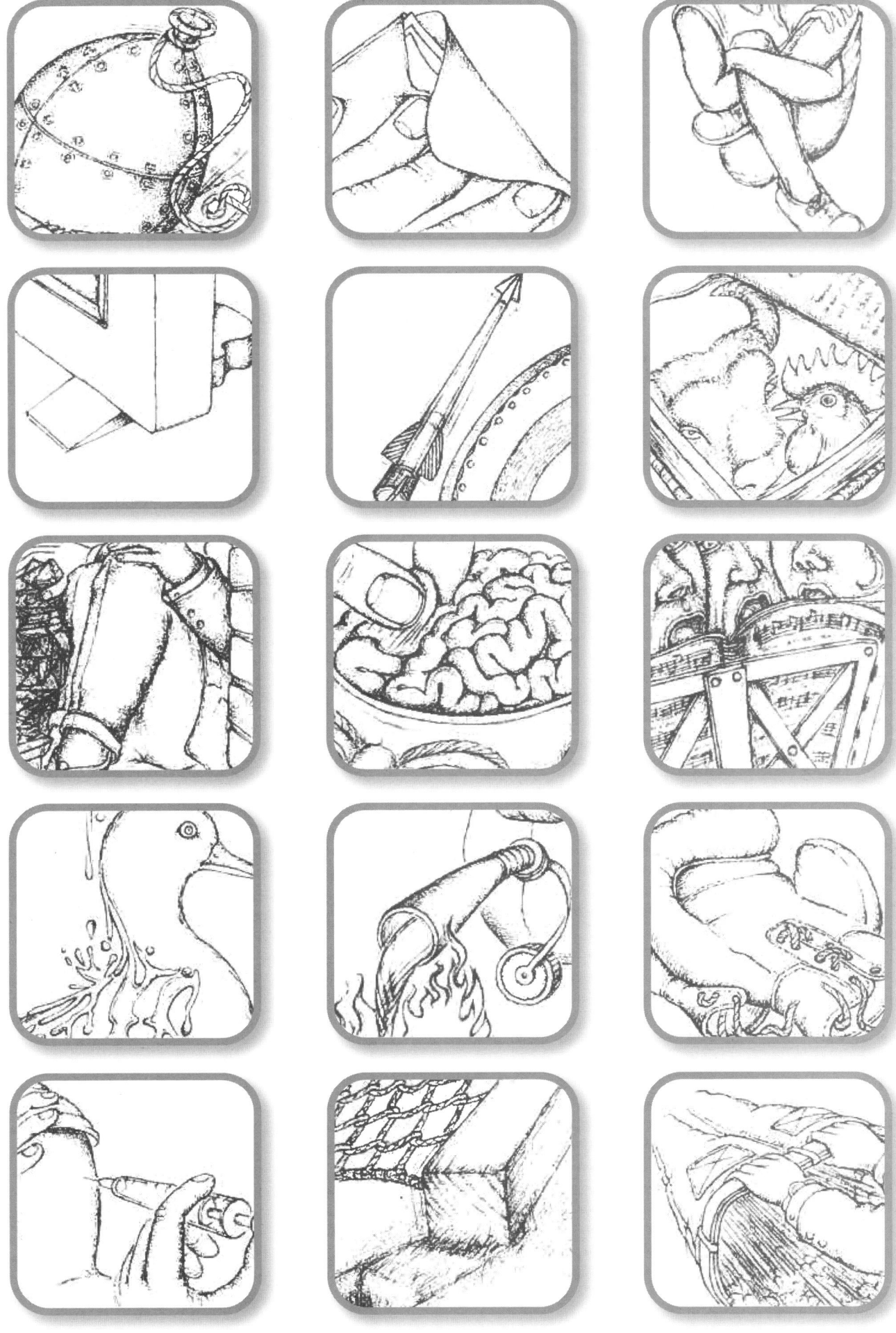

Tie yourself in knots	Push the envelope	Go down like a lead balloon
A cock and bull story	Wide of the mark	The thin end of the wedge
Sing from the same song sheet	Pick someone's brains	Between a rock and a hard place
The gloves are off	Add fuel to the fire	Water off a duck's back
Fly by the seat of your pants	Move the goalposts	A shot in the arm

a comment or suggestion which is not received well	extend the limits of performance	become very confused when you try to explain something
the start of a bigger, more harmful development	be wrong about something	a story or explanation which is obviously untrue
having to make a choice between two unpleasant options	ask advice from someone more knowledgeable	present a united front
criticism which has no effect on somebody	make an argument or bad situation worse	something will be resolved in an unpleasant way
give encouragement/ boost morale	change the rules unfairly	make decisions as you go along, without a plan

Read all about it

Microsoft layoffs add more fuel to H-1B fire

Layoff announcements by IT vendors came fast and furious over the past two weeks. But it was Microsoft Corp.'s that drew the attention of a U.S. senator, who said it was 'imperative' that the company give job priority to U.S. citizens over foreigners with H-1B visas.

"Microsoft has a moral obligation to protect ... American workers by putting them first during these difficult economic times," Senator Charles Grassley (R-Iowa) wrote in a letter to Microsoft CEO Steve Ballmer on 22 January.

IT World 2 February, 2009

Organising governing bodies

'Sing from the same song sheet' is what we all want our governing bodies to do. But well-organised groups such as these are few and far between, often because the 'song sheet' for boards is a Board Policies Manual (BPM) and most of us have an aversion to 'manuals'.

A good BPM:
- provides the ability to quickly orient new board members to current policies
- eliminates redundant, or conflicting, policies over time
- eases the reviewing of current policies
- gives clear, pro-active policies to guide the CEO and staff .

Business Bugle 4 July, 2009

Bonuses still with us

Some companies say deteriorating conditions in the capital markets and the broader economy pushed performance goals out of reach, making bonuses useless as a motivational and retentive measure.

But experts say that executives have been benefiting from a strong economy for the past several years, so that **moving the goalposts** now undermines the purpose of performance-based pay. As a result, some companies are handing out payments even though their executives might not have qualified for performance rewards.

Business Break 27 February, 2009

Shot in the arm from online finance

Nowadays, business financing is available on line. This makes life much easier for small businesses looking for quick working capital, especially those which have a history of bad credit.

Business Bugle 5 April, 2009

Job cuts fear

Scottish further education colleges are protesting about budget cuts that, they warn, will seriously hamper the recovery of the Scottish economy. Education trade unions said they fear that job losses at one college could represent the **thin end of the wedge** and told government ministers to act now to avoid a meltdown in the sector.

Northern Reporter 15 February, 2009

Caught between a rock and a hard place

Unhappy in your job? Now is not the time to make rash decisions; you're lucky to have a job at all. However the stress, depression, and overall unhappiness it may be causing you can be detrimental to your physical, mental or emotional health, as well as your productivity and your leisure time. Changing jobs is risky – many companies still operate the 'last in, first out' strategy, so you just can't win either way.

Wordsweek 23 February, 2009

Pick the brains of your 'career idols'

To 'get on' in your career, try finding someone who's just a few years ahead of you on the career ladder. Then you need to try to engineer a meeting:
- Write a short e-mail introduction. Ask them if you can pick their brain for 15-30 minutes whenever and wherever it's convenient for them.
- If they do agree to meet, ask them what education and training they had, and what their first job in the industry was.
- Be considerate of their time, and send a thank you email afterwards.
- If you're meeting over food or drinks, be sure to pick up the bill.

Weekly Bizround 23 March, 2009

Police reject man's assassination confession

A middle-aged man who 'confessed' yesterday to conspiring to murder the Prime Minister was released from custody today - after intensive questioning police rejected his claim as a **'cock and bull story'**, saying that he would not be charged with wasting police time as he was a serial fantasist who needed medical help.

Weekly Informer 21 January, 2008

Pros and cons of social networking

Most businesses want their employees to master social networking. After all, your staff are brand ambassadors for your products or services. However, the risk of breaching confidentiality has recently become a concern for senior executives. As a result, they are **tying themselves in knots** over how to handle this. Many are using new software to scour the internet to discover who or what is being talked about.

Business Break 13 March, 2009

Flying by the seat of their pants

The business model of the entire aviation industry is virtually non-existent. Since the end of January, the cost of aviation fuel has risen by almost 60 per cent. Many airlines have introduced new baggage fees, as well as a variety of other service charges, to generate hundreds of millions of pounds in extra revenue. But no-one knows if it will be enough to keep the creditors at bay.

Business Break 2 September, 2009

GM crops get the thumbs down

A recent survey has revealed that genetically modified (GM) crops are deeply unpopular. Their introduction in Britain will **go down like a lead balloon**, being seen as a threat to local foods and the environment. Councils throughout the country acknowledge this problem and are taking steps to protect their areas before it's too late. GM crops will benefit no one except the biotechnological industry.

Daily Discoverer
8 December, 2008

Bad news for the lower paid

Increasing numbers of employers in the United States are flouting long-established laws and standards designed to protect workers. In some cases, this even includes paying less than the minimum wage. No longer confined to illegal sweatshops and shady businesses, this **'gloves-off'** economy is impacting on every aspect of the low-wage labour market.

The Chronicler 28 October, 2008

Sign of the times

Do you ever become irate when you get a call from a total stranger - a 16-year old insurance salesman over the phone, for example – who asks you what kind of day you are having, or how you are? You just know this is a sweetener for the inevitable sales pitch.

These people have been sent to charm school, but most people regard their familiarity as impertinent and intrusive. Deflect the questions with sarcasm. Let what they say bounce off you like **water off a duck's back**. Laugh. Worse things happen in the world.

The Chronicler 18 February, 2009

Students' wage expectations wide of the mark

Full-time students tend to overestimate their starting salary by around 10 per cent. The most unrealistic groups tend to be those studying for a language degree, or ones who attend the 'new', or post-1992, universities. On the other hand, part-time students (that is, those who are already working part time) and those studying degrees in education have more accurate expectations, and could even be underestimating the value of their degree.

People's Courier
2 November, 2008

Creating direct mail – pushing the envelope

The envelope is a key factor in making a good first impression. It should be distinctive and recognisable, yet it is often the last thing groups consider when they are planning a mailshot. Although a lot of time and money is spent on purchasing mailing lists to ensure your direct mail is sent to the right people at the right addresses, it is at least as important to make every effort to create a strong visual impact for the recipients. This will give you the best possible chance of it being opened and read.

Business Bugle 12 May, 2009

Exercises

1 John is having a meeting with his boss. Which idioms could be used to describe John's thoughts?

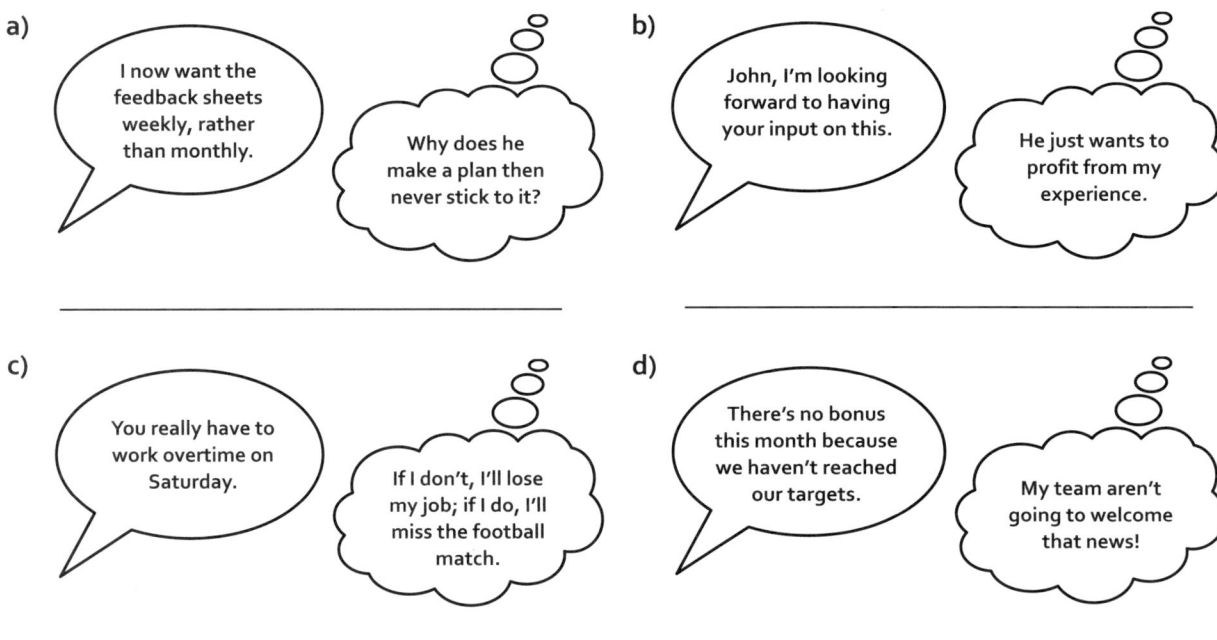

a)

> I now want the feedback sheets weekly, rather than monthly.

Why does he make a plan then never stick to it?

_____

b)

> John, I'm looking forward to having your input on this.

He just wants to profit from my experience.

_____

c)

> You really have to work overtime on Saturday.

If I don't, I'll lose my job; if I do, I'll miss the football match.

_____

d)

> There's no bonus this month because we haven't reached our targets.

My team aren't going to welcome that news!

_____

2 In the job enquiry below, the writer has used some idiomatic expressions. Is the style appropriate? Why/why not? Rewrite the letter, keeping the meaning the same, but without the idioms.

Sales Director
Garner Ltd

Dear Sir or Madam,

I am writing to enquire about sales opportunities in your company. My current employers are making radical cutbacks and to **add fuel to the fire**, our customer base has increased dramatically. My sales force are **tying themselves in knots** to maintain a high level of service for our customers.

I have worked for this organization for three years, and in that time my team and I have increased the total sales turnover of the company by 35 per cent. I have a good, supportive team who all **sing from the same song sheet**, and I know that the recent cutbacks are the **thin end of the wedge**. Any attempt to explain our difficulties to the company directors is like **water off a duck's back** – so I'm afraid **the gloves are now off**.

I am motivated and used to managing a team, and feel that I have a lot to offer your organization. I have enclosed my CV and look forward to hearing from you.

Yours faithfully,

Chris Spruce (Key Account Manager)

_____

_____

_____

_____

_____

_____

_____

_____

_____

_____

_____

_____

_____

_____

_____

3 **Discussion.**

a) Is it always necessary to push the envelope if you want to achieve recognition in your job?

b) You have to give an important presentation. What can you do to avoid tying yourself in knots on the big day?

c) What are some of the reasons for sales predictions being wide of the mark?

d) Have you ever been told a cock and bull story?

e) Name a few achievements which have given you a shot in the arm.

f) People in high pressure jobs often have to fly by the seat of their pants. What are the pros and cons of this?

Eat humble pie

In the 14th century, *numbles* was the name given to the heart, liver, entrails, etc., of animals – especially deer – and is what we now call *offal*. By the 15th century, this had become *umbles*, although the words co-existed for some time. Umbles were used as an ingredient in pies. A *numble* pie could easily have become an *umble* pie through linkage in spoken English (known as metanalysis).

Idiom summary

Breathe down someone's neck: irritate someone by checking constantly what they are doing

A square peg in a round hole: a person in a situation unsuited to their abilities or character

Off the hook: escape from a difficult situation or problem

A fly on the wall: an unnoticed observer of another situation

Hit the jackpot: have an unexpected success, often financial

Let the cat out of the bag: carelessly reveal secret information

The penny has dropped: eventually understand something

Pull the plug: put a stop to something

Feather your (own) nest: make money at the expense of other people

Pull strings: use your influence to someone's advantage

Wet behind the ears: someone with a lack of experience

Jump through hoops: do something difficult to achieve your objectives

Hit the buffers: a plan which fails to develop, or is stopped

From the frying pan into the fire: move from a bad situation to a worse one

Take a leaf out of someone's book: copy someone's good example

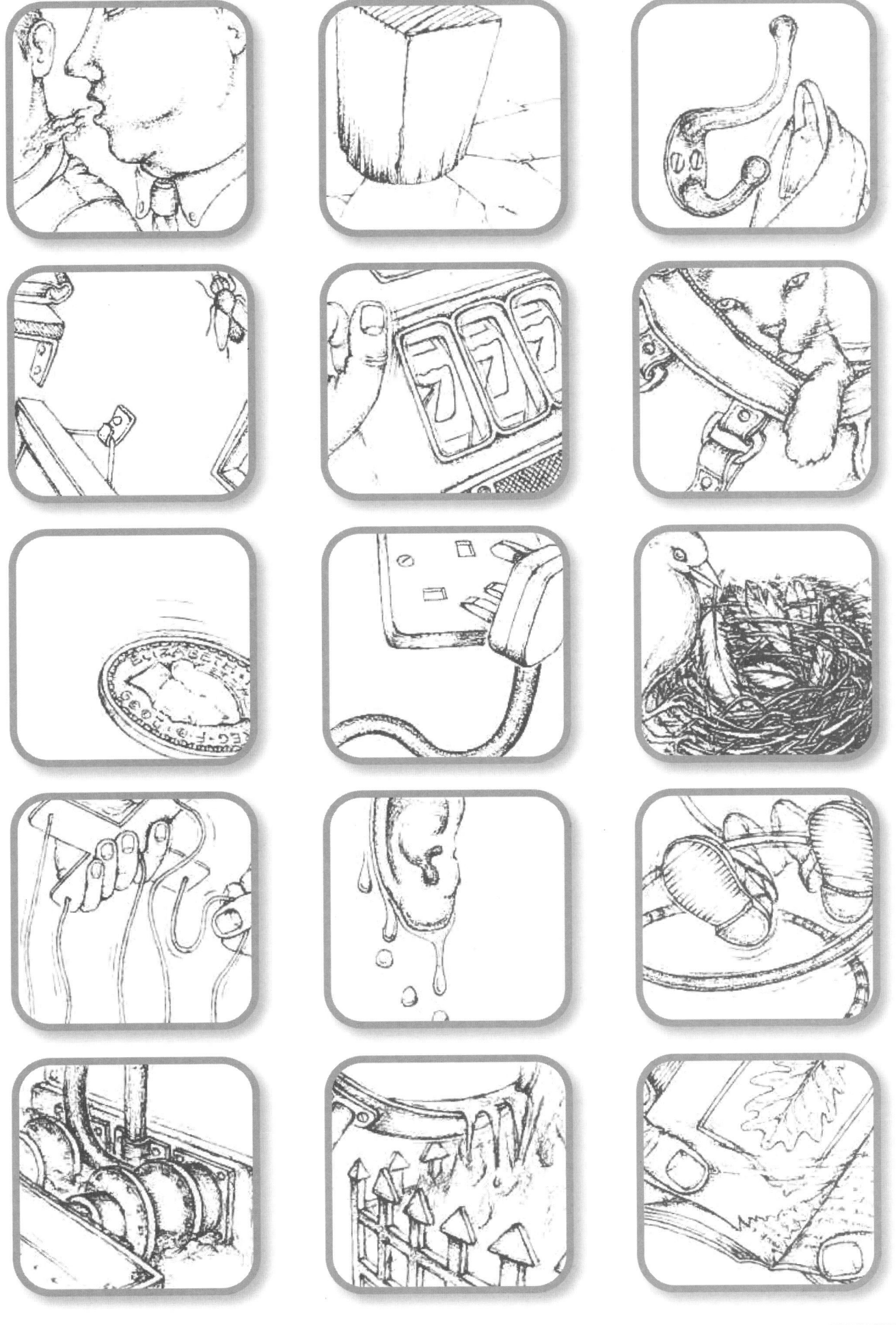

Off the hook	A square peg in a round hole	Breathe down someone's neck
Let the cat out of the bag	Hit the jackpot	A fly on the wall
Feather your (own) nest	Pull the plug	The penny has dropped
Jump through hoops	Wet behind the ears	Pull strings
Take a leaf out of someone's book	From the frying pan into the fire	Hit the buffers

irritate someone by checking constantly what they are doing	a person in a situation unsuited to their abilities or character	escape from a difficult situation or problem
an unnoticed observer of another situation	have an unexpected success, often financial	carelessly reveal secret information
eventually understand something	put a stop to something	make money at the expense of other people
use your influence to someone's advantage	someone with a lack of experience	do something difficult to achieve your objectives
a plan which fails to develop, or is stopped	move from a bad situation to a worse one	copy someone's good example

Read all about it

Try 'open house' to sell your property

Let's face it: selling your house is a lot of hassle – viewings at inconvenient times and at short notice; having to keep the house clean and tidy, and making sure your teenager's all-night party doesn't result in a houseful of sleeping adolescents as the prospective purchasers arrive. Why not get the viewings all over with in one day? As long as your estate agent advertises prominently, and someone is in attendance on the day to supervise, many people are finding that this can be a very effective way of finding a buyer quickly. Simply leave your house spic and span, go out for the day and leave the agent to it. The great advantage for the house hunter is that they will enjoy looking around the house informally, without the pressure of having an estate agent **breathing down their necks**.

Northern Weekly Chronicle 8 January, 2009

Choose a career with care

Choosing a career is not just a matter of choosing which field you want to specialise in; your personality is just as important. If you are sporty, outgoing and lively, you are unlikely to enjoy a job as a researcher, spending many isolated hours in libraries or at a computer. Your hobbies, choice of friends and even favourite styles and colours of clothes can tell you a lot about what jobs may be compatible with your personality. Failing to recognise this means you could spend great chunks of your life feeling like a **square peg in a round hole**.

National Echo 3 September, 2008

'Best-before' food seller hits jackpot

Hard times mean hard measures. People who turned up their noses at the 'budget' supermarkets are now overcoming their prejudices as the bargains they see advertised on TV become hard to ignore in the economic downturn. Similarly, companies that specialise in selling food past the best-before date have suddenly found that their time has come. Often these foods are in cans and jars and have a 'use by' date several months or even years in date, so they do not pose a health risk to the consumers. Canny customers know this, and there has been a massive rise in demand for bargains such as these.

Business Break 9 June, 2009

Oh, to be a fly on the wall

The UK's social fabric has never been better documented. If you want to understand the zeitgeist of modern Britain, watch TV. Programmes like *Hotel*, which documented the day-to-day running of a hotel with its attendant cost issues, guest problems and staff politics, drew it into the mainstream.

The fly-on-the-wall observational documentary was pioneered by the likes of people such as Roger Graef. On the plus side, the modern observational documentary goes from strength to strength. It helps you understand what it's like to be a single, resourceful mother bringing up a large family on a housing estate. Or what happens on the streets of a Midlands town on a Saturday night when the binge drinkers set off home. Or what the dynamics of modern British families can be. But on the negative side, many fly-on-the-wall documentaries have gone too far. They are cheap to produce (no actors' wages here), often pander to the extrovert misfit seeking their moment of fame, and can be tacky and tasteless. The popularity of the quintessential fly-on-the-wall show *Big Brother* has already fallen dramatically in the ratings. What will be the next fashionable genre for TV?

People's Courier 5 November, 2009

The penny has dropped

In the last year, oil prices have reached record highs – and also been their lowest in four years. **The penny has dropped** for most governments across the globe. At last they are now acknowledging publicly, many for the first time, that decreasing reliance on imported oil is becoming a necessary part of any energy policy.

Daily Focus 3 January, 2009

Pull the plug on terminally-ill businesses

Fearing for their own jobs, those employed in retail, construction and other sectors ask why banks and their employees should be subsidised by the government – and why mismanaging bosses should be bailed out.

Spending taxpayer money to keep them on life support traps workers in dead-end, subsidised jobs and squanders precious resources on businesses which (we now know) were already struggling before the economic downturn. It is a fact of economic downturns that they – necessarily in most cases - accelerate the inevitable demise of terminally ill businesses.

Soapbox 18 March, 2009

Don't stray too far when diversifying

Should you diversify in a recession? Done the right way, it can be a good way of generating additional income for your business. But you need to consider the costs carefully, as it can be a case of **out of the frying pan into the fire**, resulting in a terrible waste of time, money and effort.

Business Break 23 March, 2009

Premature press release gets photographers buzzing

Yesterday the camera company Click accidentally posted a press release announcing a significant addition to its line of digital SLR cameras. The press release was only on the web for half an hour, but that was enough to **let the cat out of the bag**. The new model is more compact and will offer a better resolution than any professional camera currently on the market. The press release wasn't supposed to reach the Web until just before the National Digital Camera tradeshow, where the product will be officially unveiled.

Although they won't discuss the details at this stage, Click has acknowledged that the release, though prematurely posted, was accurate.

Business Break 16 May, 2009

Spin doctors pull strings

Like master puppeteers, political spin doctors have been content over the years to remain behind the curtain, quietly influencing many of the government officials they helped elect.

Usually you don't get to know the individuals' names, but these men **pulling the strings** affect your daily life, from determining if the fields down the street will become a major development site, to how your taxes are spent.

National Grapevine 28 April, 2009

Locals speak out about flood prevention

Residents have spoken out against their local council, which is holding off on flood remedial works in one of the area's worst flooding hot spots, despite a report slamming the drainage and warning of expensive damage during severe downpours.

Angry residents are demanding action now and not after the wet season, which is predicted to be one of the worst on record.

"There is no room for someone **wet behind the ears**", a spokesman said, "They have enough reports and lists, and if they don't know where the hot spots are by now, then they might as well give up."

Northern Reporter 23 February, 2009

Simplify your website

Getting your website up and running is only the beginning. Most site owners, designers and webmasters don't realize how much more a site could sell, if only it were more user-friendly.

Try to make the information needed to complete a transaction within easy access of your customers, with minimal mouse clicks.

A FAQ (Frequently Asked Questions) section is good, but some prospects may still have additional questions not covered in it. You need to have an efficient system in place for answering them, promptly and efficiently.

What forms of payment do you offer your customers? If you're selling online and not accepting credit cards, you're likely to lose many sales. Also consider offering options to order by cheque, money order, or debit card, by phone, fax, or post.

Don't make your customers **jump through hoops**. Are your order forms simple to use and understand, or confusing and inconvenient to use, even for the most inexperienced users? How do you know? Aim to guide customers simply and gently through the ordering process.

Remember - there is always room for improvement.

Business Break 29 January, 2009

Working Time Directive meets with opposition

UK business leaders breathed a sigh of relief recently when EU negotiations on amendments to the Working Time Directive **hit the buffers**. The EC set up the Working Time Directive in 1993 to work alongside member states to regulate employment and health and safety laws. The UK government is also convinced that the EU's Working Time Directive is harmful to British business. An EU limit on the hours junior doctors can work comes into force on Saturday, and medical groups warn it could affect their training and ultimately jeopardise patient care.

The European Working Time Directive prevents junior doctors from working more than 48 hours a week.

Economics Daily 1 August, 2009

Facebook taking a leaf out of Twitter's book?

Facebook has now implemented a new search feature that is said to give Twitter a run for its money. Today they announced an upgrade to its search function that lets users search other people's status updates, photos, links, videos and notes, in a similar way to how the Twitter format works.

"Last month, we began testing new versions of Search with a small group of people on Facebook," the company said. "Based on the success of those tests, we're rolling out a new version of Search to everyone on the site, beginning today."

The Chronicler 11 August, 2009

Look after your future

If you are hoping to **feather your nest** for your retirement, it is crucial to plan carefully to take advantage of any tax breaks which are on offer. If you save in a company or personal pension scheme, you get tax relief on all contributions at the highest rate of income tax you normally pay. If you are already in a pension scheme, you should check what it offers and whether it would be worthwhile paying in more. You can purchase private pensions, but these often carry high charges, and you cannot take the cash at retirement as part of a lump sum – it has to be used towards a pension.

The disadvantage with pension plans are that you cannot draw from your fund to meet emergency expenses and you have to decide on a retirement date when you take out the policy. Look for a scheme allowing for early retirement without penalty - a lot of pensions will charge penalties if you want to retire early.

Many people in the UK feel that their home is their best investment, so home improvement loans could be money well spent. If you have paid off your mortgage, you can release some of the equity in your home to fund other things you need, such as hospital and other unexpected bills.

National Grapevine 5 August, 2009

Exercises

1 Tick (✓) the box if the idioms are correct. If the idioms are incorrect, rewrite them.

a) We've run out of money so we'll have to push the plug on the project. ❑

_____

b) It's confidential, so please don't let the cat out of the sack. ❑

_____

c) We've really hit the jackpot with this latest sale. ❑

_____

d) Don't ask Liz to do the accounts – she's too wet behind the ears. ❑

_____

e) Mike isn't happy here – he's a round peg in a square hole. ❑

_____

2 Questionnaire. Decide which option you would choose, and be prepared to justify your choice.

a) You win the lottery. Do you ...
   i) let the cat out of the bag and buy champagne for all your work colleagues?
   ii) shock your boss, by telling him you've hit the jackpot and are buying out his company?
   iii) keep it secret and feather your own nest?

b) You discover a junior member of your team has been fiddling his expenses. Do you ...
   i) breathe down his neck from now on?
   ii) dismiss him, he is a square peg in a round hole anyway?
   iii) let him off the hook?

c) There are plans to merge your department with another one. You are not happy. Do you ...
   i) take a leaf out of your boss's book and give in – it's no use fighting the system?
   ii) jump through hoops to prove to your employers that they are making the wrong decision?
   iii) do all you can to make sure the plans hit the buffers?

d) Someone who works for you asks if they can be considered for promotion. She is very good at her job. Do you ...
   i) pull strings to help her progress?
   ii) say yes, if she agrees to be a fly on the wall and report back on what your other staff are saying behind your back?
   iii) discourage her by telling her that she will be going from the frying pan into the fire?

3 Crossword. Each of the words you need are from an idiom in this section.

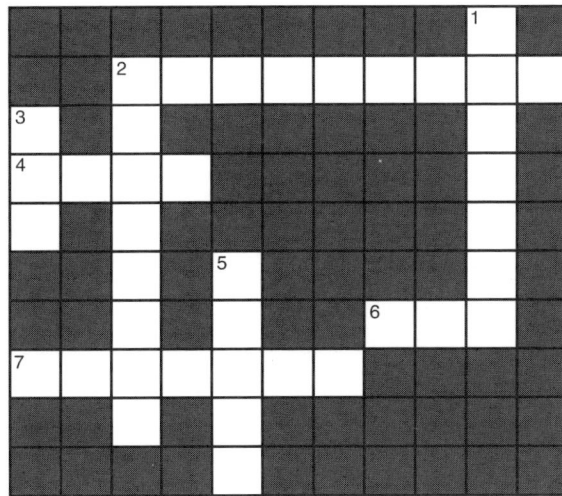

Across

2 A perfect object in which to cook your English breakfast (two words).

4 Another word for page.

6 A furry friend.

7 There are lots of these in a puppet show.

Down

1 You need a lot of luck to hit this!

2 They keep birds warm.

3 Spiders eat these.

5 There are one hundred of these in one pound sterling.

4 Discussion. In groups or with a partner, choose two topics from the list below. Decide whether you are 'for' or 'against', and make a list of points to support your argument. Then have a discussion, using as many of the idioms as possible from this section.

• The age that you can vote in a general election (18) should be lowered to 16.

• People with company cars should pay higher road tax than private car owners – after all, they use the roads much more.

• Tax havens for the rich should be abolished.

• Personal identity cards should be compulsory in all countries.

• Voluntary euthanasia should be legalized.

• Company directors who are guilty of mismanagement should forfeit their rights to a final salary pension.

Cock and bull story

Stony Stratford in England was an important stopping-off point for mail and passenger coaches travelling between London and the North of England in the 17ᵗʰ century. 'The Cock Inn' and 'The Bull Inn' were two of the main coaching inns in the town, and the banter and rivalry between groups of travellers is said to have resulted in exaggerated and fanciful stories, which became known as 'cock and bull stories'. The two hostelries did, and still do, exist.

Part C

Answer key

Section 1

1. a finger in every pie
   put all your eggs in one basket
   skating on thin ice
   drag your heels
   eat your words

2. **a)** a finger in every pie **b)** eat ~~my~~ *your* words **c)** drag your heels **d)** skating on thin ice
   e) put all your eggs in one basket

3. **a)–d)** Student's own answers **e)** bite the bullet, drag your heels/bury your head in the sand
   f)–h) Student's own answers

4. **a)** i) **b)** ii) **c)** ii) **d)** iii) **e)** iii)

5. dragging our heels, bite the bullet
   ruffle (a few) feathers, keep it under wraps
   an uphill struggle, burying our heads in the sand
   keep your hair on, bend (the boss's) ear, skating on thin ice, draw a line under it

Section 2

1. **a)** against **b)** over **c)** up **d)** in

2. **a)** break **b)** cake **c)** wires **d)** struggle

3. **i)** a spanner in the works **ii)** in the hot seat **iii)** back to square one

4. Students' own answers

5. Crossword solution

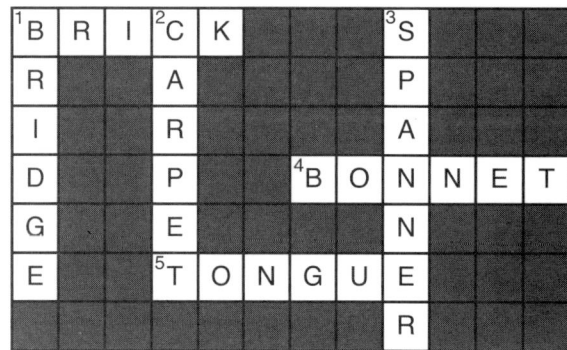

Section 3

1 **a)** mouth, holding, baby   **b)** hour, bull, horns   **c)** ball rolling   **d)** back-burner

2 **a)** jumping the gun   **b)** full of hot air   **c)** reading between the lines   **d)** splitting hairs
    e) go over the top

3 **a)** Do you have a chip on your shoulder because you didn't get that promotion?
    b) I really dislike my boss – he always picks holes in my work.
    c) I've paid through the nose for my mobile phone contract.
    d) Dave prefers to sit on the fence instead of making a decision.

4 Students' own answers

Section 4

1 **a)** throw the baby out with the bathwater   **b)** have a bone to pick   **c)** stick my neck out
    d) cut corners   **e)** open a can of worms   **f)** nail/pin (my boss) down

2 Crossword solution

3 **a)** cut corners   **b)** a hard nut to crack   **c)** puts the cart before the horse   **d)** difficult to nail/pin down
    e) play their cards close to their chest

4 Students' own answers

5 a hard nut to crack
    a big fish in a small pond
    the wrong end of the stick
    cut corners
    bite someone's head off

Section 5

1 **a)** positive   **b)** negative   **c)** negative

2 Crossword solution

3 **a)** 1   **b)** 2   **c)** 2

4 **a)** Students' own answers   **b)** a whistleblower   **c)–d)** Students' own answers

Section 6

When I started my last job they didn't tell me I would have to **make cold calls**. I was **left high and dry** because I needed the money, so I **swallowed a bitter pill** and got to work.

But to be honest, I found it difficult to **pull the wool over people's eyes** by trying to sell them something unsuitable. I would **lay my cards on the table** so that they could make an informed choice. Eventually, my boss heard about this and asked me to report to his office. I knew then that in his opinion, I had **put my foot in it**.

He said I was not working in line with company policy, so I told him that I thought his business procedures were dishonest; that I believed it was best to **put out feelers**, rather than pressurize them into buying something.

Unfortunately, he **poured cold water over** my opinions and started **shooting his mouth off**! He ended by saying that if I continued to **step out of line**, I would find myself **in at the deep end**. I knew exactly what he meant.

Hearing all this coming **straight from the horse's mouth** made me realize that I didn't want the job at all, so I resigned immediately. But there was a **sting in the tail**. The day I was due to receive my salary, it wasn't paid into my bank account. When I phoned the company to find out what had happened, they said my payment would be a couple of days late. This happened three times before I finally got paid. I was not surprised to discover that payday was **a moveable feast** because the company was having cash-flow problems. In the end, everything turned out to be a **storm in a teacup**. The job you've offered me is a much better job, and at a higher salary too!

Section 7

1 **a)** run it up the flagpole   **b)** grasp the nettle   **c)** ✓

2 **1** A   **2** C   **3** D   **4** E

3 Suggested answers: Ball is in employee's court, Union's pay claim in the bag

4 Students' own answers

5 **a** 4   **b** 6   **c** 1   **d** 2   **e** 5   **f** 3

Section 8

1 **a)** losing the thread   **b)** a glass ceiling   **c)** eat humble pie   **d)** turn up the heat
e) driving you up the wall

2 **a)** ii)   **b)** key words, i.e., nouns and verbs   **c)** Students' own answers
d) Students' own answers

3 **a)** NIP (it in the bud)
b) SCRAPE (the) BARREL
c) (a) HATCHET JOB
d) (Keep your) FEET (on the) GROUND
e) (At the) SHARP END
f) (Doesn't) HOLD WATER
g) (Strike while the) IRON (is) HOT

4 **a)** tongue   **b)** sharp   **c)** heat   **d)** record   **e)** bud

P	B	F	P	R	A	H	S
W	A	T	E	R	O	A	C
E	R	N	I	E	S	T	R
N	R	I	R	E	T	C	A
D	E	C	O	O	O	H	P
T	L	B	N	U	H	E	E
G	R	O	U	N	D	T	K
A	L	J	H	D	N	I	P

Section 9

1 **a)** always move the goalposts   **b)** pick my brains
c) between a rock and a hard place   **d)** go down like a lead balloon

2 **Suggested answer:**

I am writing to enquire about sales opportunities in your company. My current employers are making radical cutbacks **and to make things worse**, the customer base has increased dramatically. My sales force are **confused in their attempts** to maintain a high level of service for our customers.

I have worked for this organization for three years, and in that time my team and I have increased the total sales turnover of the company by 35 per cent. I have a good, supportive team who **cooperate fully with each other**, and I know that the recent cutbacks **are just the beginning**. Any attempts to explain our difficulties to the company directors are **not being received sympathetically** – so I'm afraid **the resolution to this problem may not be a pleasant one**.

I am motivated and used to managing a team, and feel that I have a lot to offer your organization. I have enclosed my CV and look forward to hearing from you.

3 Students' own answers

Section 10

1 **a)** pull the plug   **b)** cat out of the bag   **c)** ✓   **d)** ✓   **e)** a square peg in a round hole

2 Students' own answers

3 Crossword solution

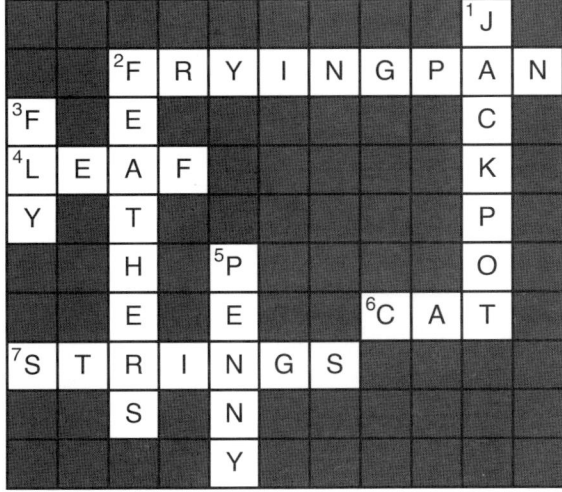

4 Students' own answers

Templates

Notes for the teacher

Templates 1, 2 and 3 can be used to create your own idiom cards.

Template 4: The student can use this to record new idioms he/she hears, with a space for writing the equivalent (if there is one) in his/her first language.

Template 5: Mind map. Write one idiom in the centre and ask the students to brainstorm other idioms which could be a) similar in meaning or b) share a key word.
For example: WET BEHIND THE EARS could result in *bend someone's **ear**, keep your **hair** on, bury your **head** in the sand, on the tip of your **tongue**, a chip on your **shoulder**, down in the **mouth**, a **foot** in the door*, and so on. Make it easier by providing students with picture cards or written idioms from throughout the book. This could be done as a team race.

Template 6: Dominoes. Split up the idioms; for example, write *Bite the* on the right-hand side of a card and *bullet* on the left-hand side of a different card, and so on.

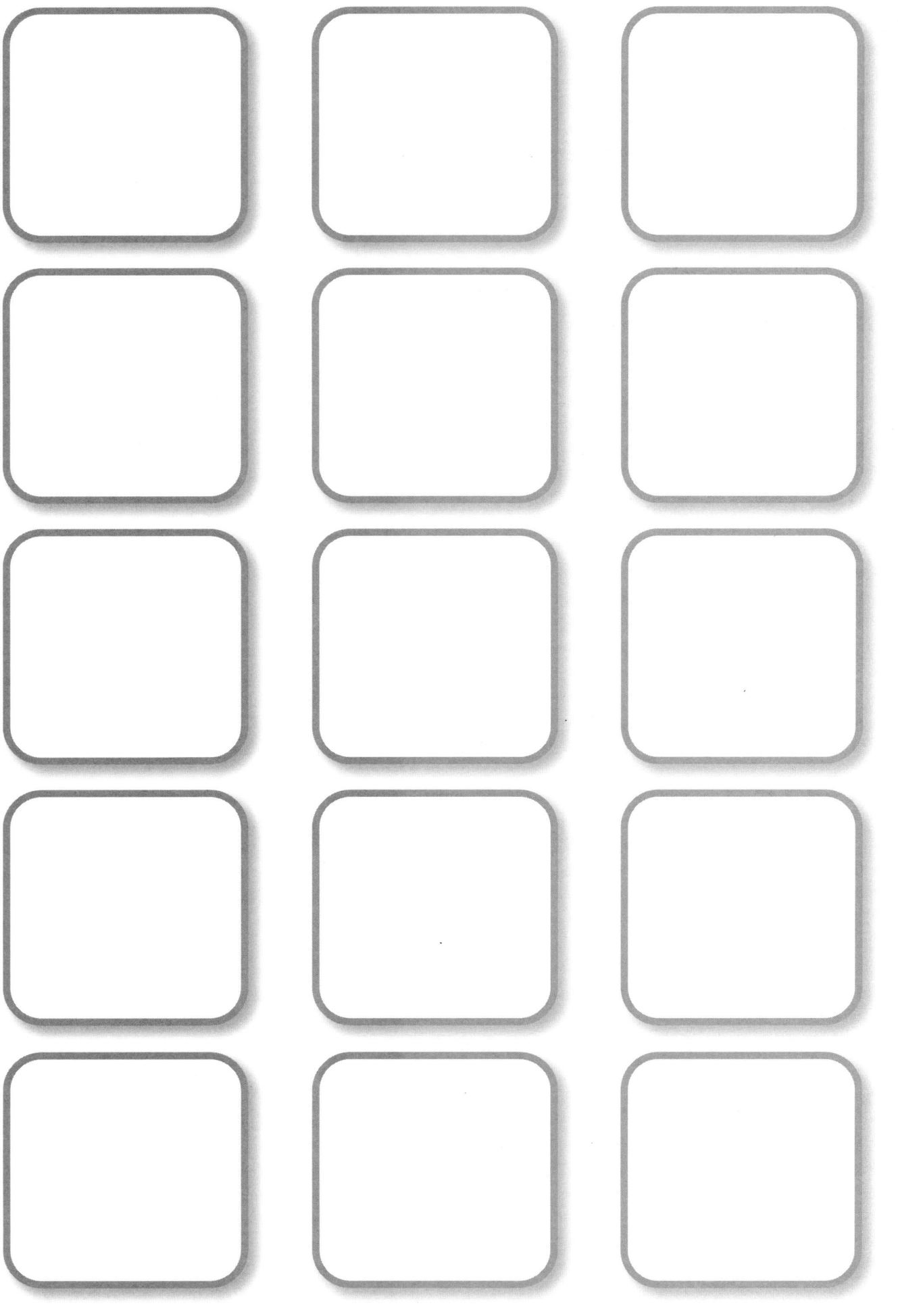

Template 4
Use this sheet to record any new idioms you hear.

Idiom	Meaning	Own language equivalent

Template 5
Mind map

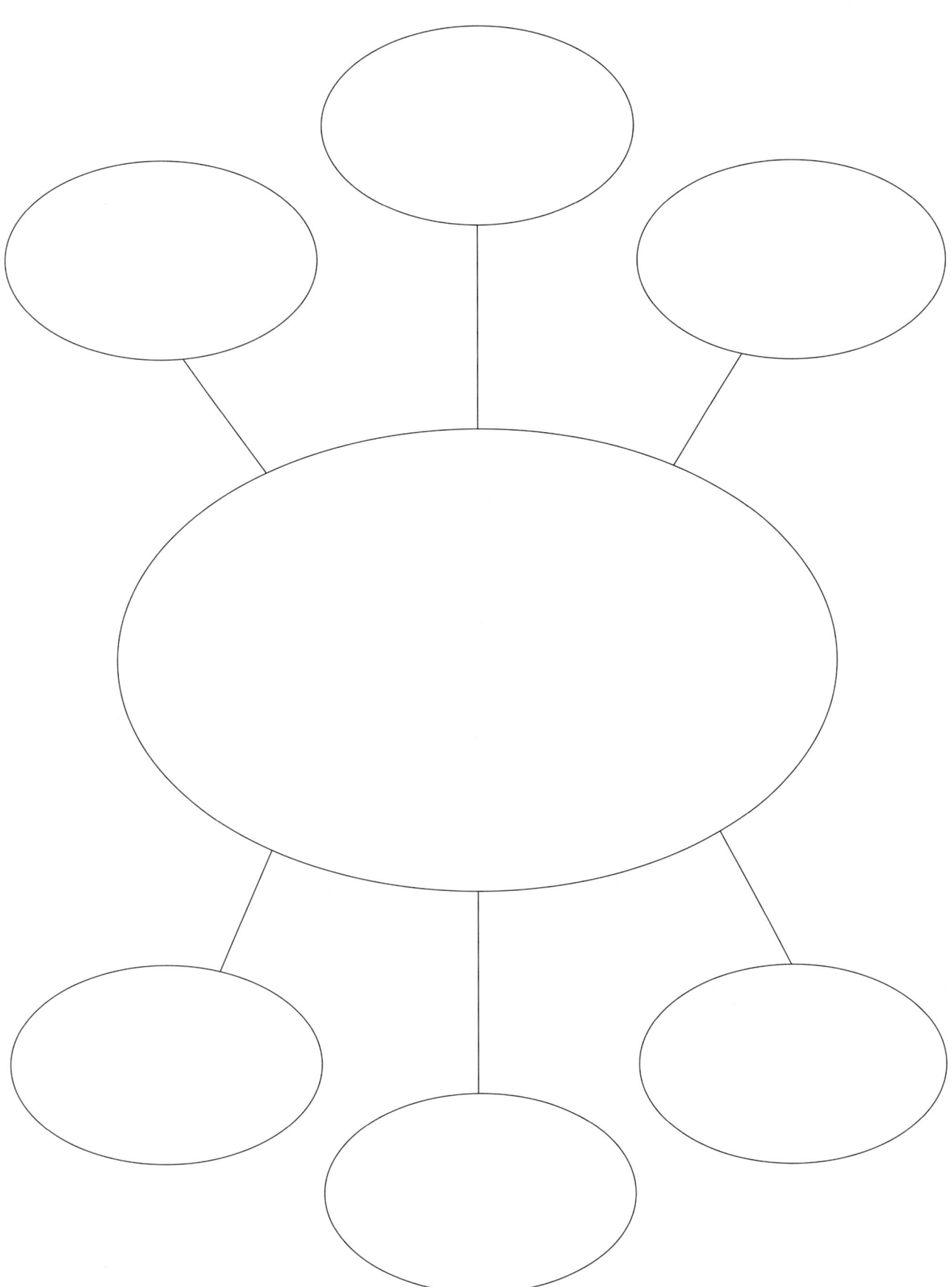

Index

	Section		Section
Hear something on the grapevine	5	**Off** the record	8
Hit the buffers	10	Go **overboard**	5
Hit the jackpot	10	**Over** the top	3
Hit the nail on the head	1	**Paint** yourself into a corner	7
From the **horse's** mouth	6	**Pay** through the nose	3
Hot under the collar	5	The **penny** has dropped	10
In the **hot** seat	2	**Pick** holes	3
In **hot** water	7	**Pick** someone's brains	9
Iron/smooth something out	4	**Pie** in the sky	5
Jump the gun	3	A **piece** of cake	2
Jump through hoops	10	**Play/keep** your cards close to your chest	4
Keep something under wraps	1	**Pour/throw** cold water over something	6
Keep your feet on the ground	8	**Pull** strings	10
Keep your hair on	1	**Pull** the plug	10
A **knee-jerk** reaction	5	**Pull** the wool over someone's eyes	6
The **last** straw	7	**Push** the envelope	9
Lay your cards on the table	6	**Put** all your eggs in one basket	1
Go down like a **lead** balloon	9	**Put** out feelers	6
Left high and dry	6	**Put** something on the back-burner	3
Left holding the baby	3	**Put** the cart before the horse	4
Let sleeping dogs lie	5	**Put** your foot in it	6
Let the cat out of the bag	10	**Read** between the lines	3
In the **loop**	7	**Rise** to the bait	7
Lose the thread	8	**Ruffle** someone's feathers	1
Make a mountain out of a molehill	1	**Run** it up the flagpole	7
Money for old rope	5	**Scrape** the barrel	8
Move the goalposts	9	At the **sharp** end	8
A **moveable** feast	6	**Shoot** your mouth off	6
Nail/pin someone down	4	A **shot** in the arm	9
Nip it in the bud	8	**Sing** from the same song sheet	9
In a **nutshell**	7	**Sit** on the fence	3
Off the hook	10	**Skate** on thin ice	1

Southampton Language College
1 Brunswick Place
Southampton
Hampshire SO15 2AN